D1444655

ORACLES

Donald N. Thompson

ORACLES

How Prediction Markets Turn
Employees into **Visionaries**

HARVARD BUSINESS REVIEW PRESS

BOSTON, MASSACHUSETTS

Copyright 2012 Harvard Business School Publishing
All rights reserved
Printed in the United States of America
10 9 8 7 6 5 4 3 2 1

No part of this publication may be reproduced, stored in or introduced into a retrieval
system, or transmitted, in any form, or by any means (electronic, mechanical, photo-
copying, recording, or otherwise), without the prior permission of the publisher.
Requests for permission should be directed to permissions@hbsp.harvard.edu, or mailed
to Permissions, Harvard Business School Publishing, 60 Harvard Way, Boston, Massachusetts 02163.

Library of Congress Cataloging-in-Publication Data

Thompson, Donald N.
    Oracles : how prediction markets turn employees into visionaries /
Donald N. Thompson.
        p. cm.
    ISBN 978–1-4221–8317-5 (alk. paper)
    1. Business forecasting. 2. Decision making. 3. Strategic planning. 4. Organi-
zational behavior. 5. Organizational effectiveness. 6. Creative ability in business.
I. Title.
    HD30.27.T566 2012
    658.4'0355—dc23

                                                                    2011053283

The paper used in this publication meets the requirements of the American National
Standard for Permanence of Paper for Publications and Documents in Libraries and
Archives Z39.48-1992.

Contents

Contents

Part Four
Making Markets Work

Prediction is very difficult, especially if it's about the future.

    —Niels Bohr, Nobel laureate in physics (sometimes credited as an
      ancient Chinese proverb)

I don't believe it is possible to make an organization more innovative without producing some pretty big changes in it. If people do things the way they always have, no amount of "creativity juice" is going to spur innovation.

    —John P. Kotter, management guru, Harvard Business School

PART ONE

Predictions from Markets

1

The Mutual Fun Market

When technologies and markets change so quickly that no manager can follow them, the most brilliant insights tend to come from people other than senior management, so we created a market to harvest collective genius.

—Jim Lavoie, CEO of Rite-Solutions

Innovation that happens from the top down tends to be orderly and dumb. Innovation that happens from the bottom up tends to be chaotic but smart.

—Curtis Carlson, CEO of SRI International

WHAT WOULD AN ORGANIZATION look like that chose prediction market democracy—that tried to solve its problems by operating on the principle that the market is smarter than the individual? Every senior executive knows that employees who interact directly with customers are the first to learn about product shortcomings and among the first to learn about competitors' tactics. Executives know that other valuable information is scattered around the organization. They just don't know how to retrieve it.

The problem is that the CEO and senior managers at the apex of the organizational pyramid are expected to be the smartest people in the room and to have the right answers. Midlevel employees possess skills, but do they understand the big picture? Using employees to evaluate new products or to choose among technologies or strategies may evoke a raised eyebrow and a mumbled "lowest common denominator."

In an organization that chooses prediction market democracy, an employee might log on to the company's intranet each day after breakfast to make a few predictive trades before heading to work. The software interface resembles that found on a Bloomberg terminal. Our employee checks her securities from the day before, considers the implications of a *Wall Street Journal* article she read over breakfast, and invests in one of five technical innovations currently under review for the company's internal development funding. She decides that predicted sales levels for a product introduced last quarter are too low, sells her earlier sales prediction of 17,500 units, and purchases one for 21,000.

Other prediction markets on her screen involve new product introductions, competitor strategies, and regional expansion. She does not consider herself knowledgeable enough about these to invest, but other employees with a better understanding of customer requirements or market trends will. That is one of the virtues of these markets: she only invests in what she knows. Unlike a survey, the market tries to gather wisdom rather than opinions. Her trades, aggregated with others, determine what actions the company will take and how it will react to daily changes in the business environment. The manager in the corner office reviews the proposed new prediction market topics, monitors the progress of existing markets, and allocates money to those projects with the greatest investor support.

Sound farfetched? Such a firm exists, and in pretty much this form. It is an information technology and engineering company called Rite-Solutions. Prediction markets can revolutionize the way companies operate. Rite-Solutions is a template for that revolution.

The company was founded in Middletown, Rhode Island, in 2000 by Jim Lavoie and Joe Marino. The two were senior executives with Analysis & Technology, a major defense contractor. In 1999, following a takeover by Anteon (which then was taken over by General Dynamics), they cashed in their stock options and left to build their own start-up company. One goal for the new Rite-Solutions was a corporate structure that would re-define what leaders do, where innovators would be freed from a hierarchy of what Lavoie calls "preventers." The two executives have achieved iconic status with those who believe in the potential of prediction markets.

Fast-forward to 2011. Rite-Solutions has 185 employees. It supplies command-and-control simulation systems for the US Navy submarines, performance measurement tools for Navy aviation combat systems, and 3D situational awareness simulations for Homeland Security—all high-tech, high-competition sectors. In the commercial market, it supplies complex player management and token-vending machines for consumers and consumer-game platforms. In the military sector, Rite-Solutions competes with multinationals General Dynamics and Lockheed Martin, and in the commercial sector with casino software suppliers IGT and Bally.

The cofounders rejected the idea that a company's direction comes from a visionary boss or inventor. Lavoie and Marino say, "We freely acknowledge that we are not the two smartest people in the company. We've got a lot of real-world experience. We've got a vision of where we want this thing to be at some point in time. But exactly how to get there, and what technologies to use, and how we should employ them—that is much bigger than any two people should be responsible for."

Instead, Rite-Solutions created an invest-in-almost-everything prediction market, which Jim Lavoie says is fun, in part because "there is no *über*-investor" telling innovators which stocks or ideas are not permissible. He says the market was designed "to take the employee relationship beyond the transaction level—I pay you, you do a job—to an emotional level where people are entrusted with the future direction of the company, asked for their opinions, listened to, recognized for their interest in the company's future, and rewarded for successful ideas." Lavoie envisioned an organization where innovation happened without his or Marino's involvement, relieving them of the burden of having to be right.

The market that implements these ideas is formally known as the Innovation Engine, less formally as the Mutual Fun Market. Any Rite-Solutions employee can propose a new product or service, a new business, a new technology, or a more efficient way of carrying out Rite-Solutions' existing business. The proposals become stocks, each with a ticker symbol and a descriptive document called an *Expect-Us*, rather than a prospectus. Each term is chosen to be playful, but also to reflect that this is a securities market.

Every employee is encouraged to take part in the market—not only engineers and computer scientists, but marketers, accountants, receptionists, and retirees. Why receptionists and retirees? Responds Lavoie, "Why would you limit intellectual bandwidth?" New employees get involved immediately—every new employee logs on to the intranet on day one and sees proposed future technologies and products and where they will be applied. Everyone invests in order to influence which initiatives receive management recognition and funding.

More important, says Lavoie, "Think about the power of what I call *knowledge tethering*. An employee who retires has tremendous intellectual bandwidth that just walks out the door. A retiree who wishes to remain relevant will jump at the chance to stay involved in a fun framework that allows his knowledge to still matter."

For help in completing the Expect-Us, the Rite-Solutions *in-ventor* (another great descriptive term) finds a "prophet," someone in the company who will support the idea and provide guidance. There may be several different prophets for each project. An undeveloped idea on an emerging technology might require a scientist prophet. As the idea takes shape and a prototype is needed, a design or marketing prophet might become involved. It is the job of the current prophet to decide when to add new prophets.

Once the Expect-Us is finished, the prophet announces an initial public stock offering (IPO), and lists the stock in one of four Mutual Fun stock markets: Savings Bonds, Bow Jones, Spazdaq, or Penny Stocks.

Savings Bonds are ideas intended to cut cost rather than increase revenue. For example, a Savings Bond with a stock ticker name *Knowledge-DNA* was suggested to automate production of Web-based courses. Administrative people are best at generating money-saving projects because they know what can be automated. As Lavoie says, "They, more than any other segment of the company, are 'waste-facing,' so who better to high-light efficiencies?"

The second stock market is the *Bow Jones*. This category is for projects that use existing technologies and competencies for new products or services. For example, employee Chuck Angell proposed using the asset-tracking technology developed for the military to monitor the location of school buses, and whether children are on the right bus.

The third market, *Spazdaq*, is for stocks that propose a technology the company might use in a new, higher risk/reward market. The fourth market is *Penny Stocks*, where employees "provide their two cents' worth of comment" and discuss blue-sky ideas that may turn into a Savings Bond, Bow Jones, or Spazdaq at some point. There is a discussion feature with every stock. It is here that investors massage the idea.

The Expect-Us and the discussion around it promote dialogue between different company offices, from Rhode Island to San Diego, among people who may never meet and may not invest in the idea but who work together to help predict the future.

Everyone in the market, including new hires, secretaries, and Lavoie, starts with $10,000 in virtual currency, called *intellectual capital*, to buy and sell Mutual Fun stocks. The price of each new security is set initially at $10. There are fifty to sixty securities listed at any one time. When employees log on to the company intranet, they see their portfolio and new offerings scroll across the screen. To buy or sell a stock, they highlight the ticker name, fill in a dollar amount, and click Buy or Sell. Most market investing takes place outside normal work hours, using a Web browser. Lavoie says it occurs "in the white space," where all innovation comes from: "The office is not always the best place for white space."

Employees can volunteer to work on any market project. The tasks needed to move the project along, called *Budge-It* items (because they budge the project), are defined and listed on the website by the prophet. The Budge-It approach hopes to capture the introverts in the organization—those who may shun the spotlight at a meeting but want to contribute without facing an "idea-kill squad." Lavoie says, "Innovation off-sites (like formal 'innovation rooms') are for extroverts. Most of your real genius is in introverts. At your off-sites, you get more theater than genius." Budge-It also allows older and younger employees the opportunity to solve problems together—with mutual respect for the other's perspective.

Lavoie and Marino have a computer display that shows the number of dollars invested in each security and the Budge-It items completed. The stock price is driven by an algorithm that takes into account the amount of investment, plus the peer group's willingness to contribute and develop the idea.

When a stock reaches top-twenty status, the prophet develops a go-forward plan and a proposal to allocate rewards. There is a financial bonus for proposing the stock, for serving as a prophet, for completing Budge-It items, or for contributing to development. Ideas that lead to savings or profit pay a dividend to the group of 25 percent of the estimated savings or profit for a two-year period. Financial bonuses are paid at the end of each year for successful investing. Smart investors also are rewarded with more money to invest; those investors gain more clout because they have proven their ability to predict well (after all, on the New York Stock Exchange, Warren Buffett has a lot more votes than I do!).

With both monetary and recognition rewards involved, the motivation to take part in the Mutual Fun Market cannot really be characterized as one or the other. The Mutual Fun Market is an integral part of the Rite-Solutions corporate culture. It is part of what each employee does. All investors know that senior officers track their involvement and success.

In the first two years of its existence, the Mutual Fun Market produced fifty innovative products, services, and process ideas. Twelve resulted in new intellectual property for the company and new patents.

The company's first successful prediction project involved 3D visualization technology—think of an X-Box—to help Navy and Homeland Security personnel make better decisions in emergency situations. When the project was first suggested, Joe Marino thought the idea, ticker name VIEW, had little potential. However, market support was strong, and VIEW was fast-tracked through development and prototype. As Marino noted: "Would this have happened if it were just up to the guys at the top? Absolutely not. But we could not ignore the fact that so many people were rallying around the idea." The resulting product, called Rite-View, accounted for 30 percent of Rite-Solutions sales the year the product launched. As the company has grown, Mutual Fun Market products have come to represent a steady 20 percent of total sales.

The Mutual Fun Market turns up new uses for existing products. Among the company's technologies are pattern-recognition algorithms for military applications that involve real-time image processing. An improbable in-ventor was a company administrative aide named Rebecca Hosch. She had no engineering background whatsoever, but thought the algorithms could be the basis of a fun game to teach history or math (or, she said, almost anything). She developed an Expect-Us, was assigned a prophet, and launched a Bow Jones stock called Win/Play/Learn, stock ticker WPL. The stock attracted both corporate investment and volunteers. Rite-Solutions spent $20,000 to develop WPL architecture, and offered the architecture to Hasbro, a Rhode Island–based toy company. Hasbro used it on its VuGo multimedia system, which launched at the beginning of 2006.

The architecture brought Rite-Solutions over $1 million in subsequent contracts. Hosch's bonus was a major portion of the 25 percent of estimated profit from the WPL architecture over the next two years.

Rite-Solutions employees then floated one of the quickest-rising stocks ever to appear on the Mutual Fun Market, the Mutual Fun Market itself (symbol STK). So many executives from other companies were asking about the system that a team championed the idea of licensing the software as a Rite-Solutions product. In mid-2006, the company launched a product called Mutual Fun, and immediately licensed it to several multinational companies. One licensee is Notre Dame University, where professor Gregory Crawford had the vision of creating a curriculum on *collab-reneurship*, using the Innovation Engine as the platform to create new businesses.

And in 2010, Rite-Solutions got a bonus from Rebecca Hosch's earlier WPL idea. Hasbro was intrigued with Mutual Fun, liked what they saw, and asked that it be redone with Hasbro's own *Monopoly* theme as the graphical user interface. A product called Idea Monopoly was launched in late 2011.

The key to the success of the company's prediction market process is their corporate culture. There is no executive veto on new ideas. With Rite-Solutions, the culture is everything. Its hiring process is described as a "tryout" to find "partners in our culture." Most new employees get their first interview through referrals from existing employees. They must have technical competence, but they must also be "someone I would want to share an office with."

Every employee has heard Jim Lavoie say how much he dislikes the idea of the traditional pyramidal organization structure. A pyramid, says Lavoie, is "a tomb for dead people; it is especially seen as a tomb by the Y Generation entering the workforce, where the old norms associated with command and control in a hierarchical pyramid organization are irrelevant." An organizational box, he says, "is a temporary storage bin where people box with others until they land in another temporary box and box new people for the next box for dead people stuck in a pyramid."

Worst of all, says Lavoie, "the perception is that with a pyramid, people at each level are smarter than those below them." Lavoie dislikes the structure not only because it inhibits input from those lower in the pyramid, but also because it puts pressure on people at the top to always be right. Opening up the process to every employee produces useful ideas—and products such as Win/Play/Learn. Lavoie says of that innovation, "This product never would have occurred to management. Respect and implement your people's intellectual capital investments and monitor their momentum, even when it contradicts senior management thinking."

Is it worthwhile to bypass the pyramid, to give up the certainty of a CEO who is the smartest guy in the room, for a Mutual Fun Market? Charles Leadbeater, author of *We-Think: The Power of Mass Creativity*, says, "If you are locked into the power in certain parts of your company and are not willing to look anywhere else, you are probably ignoring some great ideas. If one company ignores them, another won't."

Rite-Solutions illustrates the basic idea behind a prediction market. Useful information is spread among a great many people. Even when investors are not experts—and often because they are not experts—prediction markets do a great job of producing a good collective judgment. Traders face none of the barriers that prevent the flow of information and the making of unbiased decisions. There is no one to offend and no watchdog dictating what is politically correct.

Rite-Solutions makes a fascinating case study. There are other case studies in this book, but prediction markets are far more than good stories. This is potentially a social revolution. Prediction markets can replace surveys or substitute for endless meetings. They can also change your life, change your company or organization, and change society. With each of the stories that follow, go beyond "Aha!" and ask, "What does this mean? What does this say about what I do, about what my company does, about how my government works? How can markets improve those things?"

I was familiar with some prediction markets when I began the journey of discovery that became this book. The more I learned about how markets were being used to aggregate the wisdom in groups, the more enthusiastic I became with the possibilities. Markets have been used to select the lead in a Broadway musical, to predict the delay in delivery of the Boeing 787 Dreamliner months before the CEO of the company was told of it, and to accurately forecast US presidential elections. Retailers use them to select what products to carry and how to price and promote. Technology firms use them to decide what new platforms to invest in. And Hollywood movie studios use markets to decide how much money to spend on advertising campaigns for new films.

For many companies, prediction markets have remained an interesting curiosity. But operating under-the-radar, a number of innovative organizations—General Electric and Google, Motorola and Microsoft, Hewlett-Packard and Eli Lilly, even the Central Intelligence Agency—have used markets to make better decisions and to allow employees to become visionaries. Prediction markets may be the most important technique that most managers have never tried to understand.

2

What Are These Prediction Markets?

None of us is as smart as all of us.

—Japanese proverb

PREDICTION MARKETS IN THEIR various forms are one of the least understood ideas in business. Even though some of the examples that appear later in this book have been mentioned in the *Economist, National Geographic, Time,* and major business newspapers, few readers would associate prediction markets with the applications used by Rite-Solutions, or with Google, or with predicting flu epidemics.

There is a long history to the prediction-making business. In Greek mythology, the first source of predictions—the earliest oracle—was Gaia, the earth goddess. She dwelled at Delphi on the slopes of Mount Parnassus, dispensing profound wisdom and foretelling the actions of gods and kings. Without the benefit of a twenty-first-century Gaia, businesses and governments must predict what will happen tomorrow, next month, or next year. Even where cross-functional teams and open feedback systems exist, business organizations are bad at aggregating their employees' thinking on critical issues. Overconfidence, pressure from Wall Street analysts, risk aversion, or fear that messengers bearing bad news will be shot, all conspire to reduce the flow of good information.

Securities analysts are wrong as often as they are right. Government experts failed to predict the revolution in Iran, the fall of the Berlin Wall, the resurgence of the Taliban in Afghanistan, or the 2007–2009 global credit crisis.

Maybe the record is spotty because future events really are unpredictable, too random. Or the prediction is unsuccessful because traditional predictive methods are unreliable. Maybe instead of relying on specialists or experts, we should try something else—like aggregating the collective wisdom of a large number of people. To do this, businesses and organizations experiment with prediction markets.

The first prediction market was designed by academic Robin Hanson, who is now recognized as the father of these markets. Hanson was consulting for a company called Xanadu, and looking for a strong topic for a test market. In April 1989, a controversy erupted in the physics community over a reported discovery of cold fusion by two University of Utah physicists. Hanson asked Xanadu employees and consultants to evaluate the following statement:

> By January 1, 1991, a less than one liter device will have
> generated over one watt of power output more than input
> from room temperature fusion, including amortized power to
> create/separate components.

Translation: Cold fusion will actually generate electricity.

Eighteen people took part in this first corporate market question. The opening probability was above 50 percent, reflecting excited news reporting of the Utah experiment. By May 1990, it had dropped to 6 percent. The market fall came well before scientific opinion had coalesced around the conclusion that the fusion experiment could not be replicated. When the market dropped to 4 percent, it was terminated prior to its scheduled completion.

The seeds of using investors as predictors had been sown. Prediction markets now take a variety of forms. Google, Best Buy, and Microsoft have markets to estimate product-sales levels and new project launch dates. Commercial prediction markets include the Iowa Electronic Markets (IEM) and the Irish company Intrade. These markets offer securities on everything from stock prices and election outcomes to the spread of epidemics.

There are also unconscious prediction markets. When you leave your cell phone turned on, the service provider can track your movements. Research firms can then use this information to predict what form of transportation people like you will use—or the bars you will visit after a baseball game. When you go on Google and access articles on flu symptoms, researchers aggregate your information with that of others to track the geographic spread of disease. There are also less-known markets providing information to governments on terrorism and assassination.

One reason you may not have heard much about corporate prediction markets is that executives who use them are reluctant to admit that some decisions come in part from secretaries and technicians. Check annual reports or corporate websites of Microsoft, Yahoo!, General Electric, Hewlett-Packard, Motorola, General Mills, or any of the other sixty major corporations now running internal markets and see if you can find a single mention of the technique. Google and Best Buy have each had their internal markets discussed and praised in the business press. Neither company mentions markets in its annual report or on its website. John Delaney of Intrade once predicted that when you first read in an annual report about the success of a corporate market and how much it produced in savings, it will signal that the technique has come out of the closet and been embraced and legitimized by the corporate world.

We readily accept market consensus in other forms. The price of a security on the New York Stock Exchange reflects the aggregated wisdom of thousands of investors and hundreds of mutual fund managers, all condensed into a single price for a share of that stock. The price reflects predictions on a bundle of things: the firm's business strategy, its marketing abilities, its underlying technologies, and future demand for its products. Mutual funds are purchased by individuals who think fund managers can make better predictions on these bundles of ideas than they can.

The price estimate for the security (or a share in the mutual fund) is not perfect, but the market is better than any other technique we have for estimating it.

Similarly, commodity market prices represent a prediction of future demand for, among other things, wheat, corn, oil, or gold. Commodity prices also reflect a bundle of ideas—the effects of weather, political stability, disruption from piracy or wars, and what interest rate will be set by the Bank of China. The purpose of a commodity market is to transfer ownership. The secondary effect is to provide aggregated information.

Prediction markets turn the side effect of a market into the main effect. An aircraft manufacturer that wants to know whether a new plane will be delivered on time can set up a market for employees and contractors to invest on the question, "Will the test flight take place by October 15?" If the current price of the security is $2 and a correct answer pays $10, that can be interpreted as a 20 percent chance of a test flight by that date.

Some investors in commodity markets buy for their own future use: corn to be turned into breakfast cereal, or jet fuel for trans-Atlantic flights. Others are speculators who don't want to take delivery of the commodities but think they have superior knowledge about the bundle and therefore about the correct price. It is participants in the speculative part of the commodities market that mirror a prediction market. Those participants keep investing until the market reaches what they consider to be the "right" price.

To understand how effective markets are, it is necessary to understand their results. What do they actually mean? The most common criticism of prediction markets is that the market predicted something would happen, and with a high probability, and it didn't. Weather reports are an example: "The weatherman predicted a 90 percent chance of rain, and it was sunny all day."

Actually, the weatherman is accurate if it rains 90 percent of the days that he gives a 90 percent prediction of rain. If it rained every time, it would mean the weatherman is *not* a good predictor.

This "weatherman misunderstanding" is the usual basis of the "I told you so" by managers who are annoyed because their judgment is being second-guessed by a market collective of lower-echelon workers.

In reality, some highly probable events always fail to materialize. Otherwise, the prediction system that declared these as "probable" is faulty. Consider the following situation. The National Basketball Association holds a yearly draft of new players. The fourteen teams with the worst season records begin with a lottery to determine draft order. The league does not simply draft in reverse order of the number of games won; that might motivate teams at the bottom to try to secure a higher draft pick by losing as many games as possible once they are sure of missing the playoffs.

Instead, the league commissioner conducts a lottery in the form of a draw. In a well-known example, the 2007–2008 Miami Heat, the NBA team with the worst season record, had a 25 percent chance of drawing the first draft pick. The Chicago Bulls, which had the ninth-worst record, had a 1.7 percent chance. Those probabilities left everyone—certainly Miami basketball fans—believing the Heat was certain to draft ahead of the Bulls.

In June 2008, against the odds, Chicago was drawn first in the league lottery, giving the Bulls first draft choice, which was used to take Derrick Rose from Memphis. Miami, with fifteen times the chance of Chicago of choosing first, drew the second pick. In 2011, Rose became the youngest player to win the NBA most valuable player award.

Was there anything suspicious about this draft result? No. In one hundred years of an NBA draft lottery, the team with the worst record can expect to be drawn twenty-five times. One of the other thirteen teams in the lottery will be drawn the other seventy-five times.

It is hard to understand how a sure thing can lose that often. But if the favorite has a 98 percent chance of winning, it will lose one time in 50. A 90 percent favorite will lose one time in ten, and an 80 percent favorite, one in five. This is why prediction market results—and all predictions—have to be wrong sometimes in order to be accurate. Unless a prediction market says "100 percent" there is never certainty of the event happening. At 100 percent, there is no point in running the market.

Think of the 2008 New Hampshire presidential primary. Hillary Clinton beat Barack Obama, even though the final pre-election aggregate of the twelve polling organizations that surveyed voters said Obama had a 67 percent chance of winning the state. Every television pundit chose Obama. Newspaper columnists then wrote for days about why the polls and pundits failed. (The answer is that on Election Day, more voters than expected, particularly more older voters, turned out.)

Another issue in understanding market results involves time. At one point, the 2008 Intrade commercial prediction market on the US presidential race gave John McCain a 52 percent chance of winning. This was not a mistake; it was a prediction of the final result if nothing else changed between the date of the market and Election Day. The election scenario, and the Intrade market, did change day-to-day with candidate gaffes, vice presidential selection, and concern about past candidate indiscretions. The Intrade market was a good estimate of McCain's chances at that one point.

The exception to that "one point" comes in the last hours of the final day of an election campaign, when investors often overestimate the chances that the behind-at-this-point party will rebound in the time remaining. Statisticians call it the Yogi Berra bias, "It ain't over 'till it's over."

So how do we judge how accurate an election market is? We judge the probability it offers at 6 p.m. the evening before the election. That is when investors in the market have incorporated all available information. We have the next-day election outcome against which to judge the market result.

To judge prediction market success, look at whether events actually happen 20 percent of the time the market predicts a 20 percent probability. Inkling, a Chicago-based prediction markets company, has illustrated how well its own markets meet this test. Inkling analysts looked at seven thousand markets that used the company's platform, counted the number of markets that had predicted something would happen 20 percent of the time, and found that close to 20 percent of those events occurred.

If markets predicted 75 percent, about 75 percent of those events occurred. Inking graphed how often events occurred against the predicted

FIGURE 2-1

Occurrence of an event and predicted probability

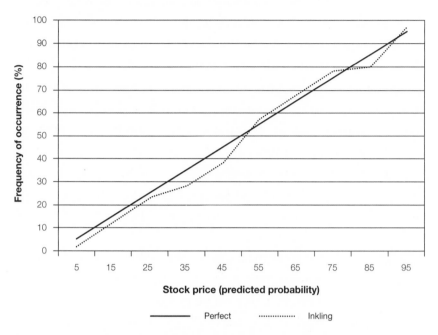

Source: Inkling corporate blog, www.inklingmarkets/home/dotheywork. Reproduced with thanks to Adam Siegel, Inkling Corporation.

probability of each event (measured by the stock price in the prediction market) and came up with the comparison depicted in figure 2-1. The straight line is what the prediction record for these markets would look like if it were perfect. The other line is what actually happened.

The markets discussed so far have predicted an event. Another type of prediction market asks the numerical outcome of something. How many men and women will apply at US Navy recruiting centers in the United States over the next thirty days? If a prediction market chose the interval "Between 12,500 and 15,000 applicants," and 13,750 actually applied, the market would be perfect. When Inkling compared numerical predictions and actual numbers in their markets over time, the results were as good as those for predicting an event.

In each of the markets represented in figure 2-1, no individual knows everything there is to know about the uncertain event. Many know very little. Allowing investors to trade with one another in a market aggregates the dispersed information. Traders who think they have good information make bigger investments and have a greater influence on stock price. Those who possess little valid information invest little.

Some of the outlier predictions may just represent someone asking *garbage-in, garbage-out* questions (known to statisticians as GIGO). These are questions where almost no investors can contribute useful information. Will Donald Trump announce his candidacy for mayor of New York City within the next three months? What city will be awarded the 2026 Football World Cup? If you pose these questions, someone will try to answer them. But the answer will be garbage-out. Markets are not a magic tool to use on haphazard events.

Logic says that a commercial market like Inkling or Intrade should produce results as good as any competing prediction method. The reason is that anyone with a superior methodology has a huge profit motivation to invest in those markets. If trades by the person with the better methodology and information don't change Intrade prices (because others keep investing against him), the individual with the better information will make a lot of money and will keep investing. In most cases, better-informed traders move the Intrade price in the direction suggested by their better methodology. Eventually Intrade will make the same predictions as whatever any better methodology might offer.

Even in cases where prediction markets are no more accurate than other forecasting tools, they have other virtues. Take an application such as forecasting whether a project's target dates will be met. Markets provide a sense of how strongly prediction views are held—an 80 percent probability of success being better than 40 percent.

Single predictions are the blunt end of the prediction market continuum. Markets offer a good way to look at "If this, then what?" conditional questions like "If coalition forces invade Iraq, what will happen to oil prices?" Asking "If this, then what?" questions usually involves creating a prediction market with two complementary questions: "How much will x

be if *y* occurs?" and "How much will *x* be if *y* does not occur?" Substitute anything you want for *x* and *y*: "The level of the S&P 500," and "Troops withdraw from Afghanistan?" or "Gas prices," and "Drilling permitted in the Arctic National Wildlife Refuge."

Think of how valuable these results could be to the political debate. Let's say a pair of markets in 2007 had predicted the S&P 500 to reach 1700 if US troops began to withdraw from Iraq but 1450 if they did not. The financial consequence the stock market attaches to US military policy is represented by an S&P 500 spread of 250 points. These linked questions let us explore issues we have no other way of investigating. What will happen to the housing market if Michele Bachmann beats Barack Obama in 2012? OK, that market might be garbage-out, at least if run a year in advance, but that is the idea of a conditional market.

Most corporate prediction markets exist just within a single organization (reasons for this can be found in "The Legal Conundrum Facing US Prediction Markets"). But this may change. Think what might happen were Rite-Solutions to extend Mutual Fun outside of its own organization to seek insights from customers, suppliers, and the military/homeland security technology community—essentially from everyone who is prepared to work with the company, even if they do not work for it. Think what Rite-Solutions might achieve if it could harvest ideas from the world military establishment.

Extending a market outside the organization is not a new idea; it was used early in the twenty-first century at drug company Eli Lilly. After several years of running an internal prediction market, Lilly funded the Inno-Centive start-up in Andover, Massachusetts. Run by Alpheus Bingham, formerly a senior research scientist at Lilly, InnoCentive was intended to connect with problem solvers outside the company.

Lilly's internal prediction market was composed of a diverse group of fifty product managers, chemists, and biologists, and was used to predict outcomes such as identifying which new drugs sent through the Food and Drug Administration's multimillion-dollar testing process would ultimately be rejected. Investors were told the molecular composition, testing protocols, and outcome of toxicology reports for each of six drugs.

They were asked to trade shares in a market to predict the three drugs most likely to receive regulatory approval.

The market correctly predicted the three successful drugs, and the three that should have been killed before tens of millions of dollars were spent on final-stage testing. Trading data revealed shades of opinion that would never have appeared under any other prediction method—a drug share at $80 reflected greater confidence than $60.

This was a great problem for an internal prediction market. Lilly knew that the scientists who developed the drug and the researchers responsible for animal and human tests had a good instinct for whether a drug would pass regulatory hurdles. But they had no incentive to tell anyone and lots of incentive not to stick their necks out. They performed their own research responsibilities and then passed the drug on to the next level in the Lilly pyramid. Failing to obtain regulatory approval was someone else's problem.

The Lilly problem, never faced in Rite-Solutions' culture, was what to do with contradictory results. If Lilly's multilayered scientific approval process said one thing and its internal market said another, which should the company go with? How do you tell scientists that a diverse set of product managers and chemists are smarter? At Rite-Solutions, this never arises because everyone just assumes the market is smarter.

Lilly had a follow-up problem that was less appropriate for an internal prediction market, so it took the problem to the InnoCentive start-up. The company was looking for a more efficient way to conduct Phase I and Phase II clinical trials of a new cancer treatment in the United States and abroad. The best input came from scientists involved in the approval process in regulatory agencies. They had plenty of ideas but had never before been given the opportunity to express them.

What happens if an investor just uses a prediction market to hedge risk? The 2008 election markets on the US presidential race provide an example. Three commercial markets on election markets—Intrade, the IEM, and Betfair—moved together after Hillary Clinton conceded in early June and Obama became the de facto Democratic candidate. The exception was a price gap that opened up on September 22. Betfair and Intrade were suddenly 10 cents apart on their Obama-to-win price: 51 cents to 61. When arbitrageurs noticed the spread, they bought at 51 and sold at 61, until the market prices came together. Arbitrageurs would earn a risk-free profit if the final Obama vote share was between those numbers. It was, and they did.

John Delaney of Intrade investigated and said that one investor had made a major investment on John McCain, large enough to move the market, to "manage certain risks." What sort of risks? Well, if the investor had purchased health-care stocks on the assumption of an Obama win, he could hedge his investment by also buying McCain securities. If Obama won, the investor made money on health care but lost his prediction market investment—and vice versa.

The actual hedger in this case may have been a company called Centrist Messenger, a firm that sells political ads and refunds money to customers whose candidate loses. Centrist has said publicly that it uses Intrade to hedge its exposure. If Centrist had sold more Obama than McCain ads, it would be overexposed to a McCain victory. It could then purchase McCain and sell Obama on Intrade.

Investing to intentionally bias the outcome of a market, say for a presidential election, could be done as a kind of strategizing. But other investors anticipate this and almost always compensate by bidding the price back to where they think it should be. In the 2004 US presidential election, one investor on Intrade spent tens of thousands of dollars to short George W. Bush presidential shares. The Bush price dropped from 54 (a 54 percent chance of reelection) to 10 (almost no chance) in eight minutes. The drop reflected four massive sell orders placed by the same individual. Six minutes later, the Bush contract was back to 54. Was this an attempt at manipulation or just a wealthy trader investing because he had a different estimate of President Bush's chances? Probably the former, but in either case the result was the same. The market price for the Bush contract returned to its original level quickly as other traders jumped in. The manipulator, if that is what he was, lost his investment.

In an experiment in the same election market, economists Koleman Strumpf of the University of North Carolina and Timothy Groseclose of

Stanford University made random investments. Strumpf says, "The market would undo what we had done in a few hours. People weren't being fooled by our crazy investments."

The Bush and Strumpf/Groseclose examples reflect what prediction market administrators refer to as the *marginal traders* idea: the existence of dispassionate traders who make money by buying or selling securities when they think the security price is wrong. Marginal traders are the Warren Buffets of the election market, investing with a less-biased view of each candidate's chances.

There is interesting research from Robin Hanson and others at George Mason University arguing that attempted market manipulation actually increases the accuracy of a real-money market like Intrade. Participants can now make a lot more money investing in the "correct" price. Hanson describes it in terms of sheep and wolves. Sheep are not very knowledgeable in their trading; wolves take advantage. Wolves prefer markets with lots of sheep. The better-informed wolves get lots to eat. Prediction markets with lots of manipulators or other sheep are more accurate. You want dumb or biased traders for the same reason you welcome a really bad poker player to sit down at your table.

Some prediction market questions are quite innovative. Movie studio executives invest in a prediction on whether a new movie will contend for an Oscar. A school board wants information on the most cost-effective way of increasing reading scores for sixth-grade students. Intelligence agencies aggregate publicly held information about the location and timing of a terrorist attack. Each example is discussed in chapter three, eleven, or twelve.

There are really only four requirements for a successful prediction market. Most important is diversity in the background and problem-solving approach of the people taking part. There must also be independent decision making by investors, with no undue influence or bullying. There must be some way of aggregating the group's information. And there must be an incentive to get people to take the exercise seriously. Incentives may be monetary, but they don't have to be.

In discussing markets I use the word *predict* rather than *forecast*. Today they have the same meaning, but not in the past. The term *forecast* originated with Captain Robert FitzRoy, the commander of Charles Darwin's historic 1831–1836 voyage around the world. FitzRoy was fascinated by the possibility that weather could be predicted, allowing for the naval office to warn vessels of an impending storm.

The weather-prediction industry of the time was made up of astrologers and almanac writers. An astrologer would predict a nonrain day to hold an outdoor event. If it did not rain, the astrologer was paid; if it rained, he was not. In Britain, this gave him about a 30 percent chance of making money on a prediction. Motivated by the possible military implications, the British government in 1854 set up a weather-prediction office for FitzRoy called *The Met*, which used the new telegraphic service to learn the direction and wind speed of existing storms.

Officials of the British Royal Society were incensed that science was being cheapened by the Met's use of the term *prediction* for something that seemed closer to astrology than to serious science. So FitzRoy invented a new word, *forecast*, to describe tomorrow's weather. The terms are now used interchangeably, but everyone involved in prediction markets uses the nonweather version.

In later chapters there are many other examples of market use: in tracking initiatives such as store openings and aircraft delivery, in sales forecasting, in quantifying risks, and in identifying innovative ideas and investment opportunities that deserve funding. But first, consider some other, better-known examples of how well markets can work—and how they do work—to aggregate the wisdom found in groups.

3

Sports and Movie Markets

Doctors and scientists predicted that breaking the four-minute mile was impossible, that one would die in the attempt. When I got up from the track after collapsing at the finish line, I figured I was dead.

　　—Roger Bannister, after becoming the first person to break the four-minute mile in 1952

Forget it. No Civil War picture ever made a nickel.

　　—MGM executive's evaluation of a script proposal for *Gone With the Wind*, which went on to become, in inflation-adjusted dollars, the highest-grossing movie of all time

HOW FAR CAN we carry the idea that a group might outpredict any of its individual members, or outperform an expert? Could novice bettors at a horse racing track out-predict professional race handicappers? Could fans placing bets on football games beat the professionals who set odds for Las Vegas casinos? Could moviegoers predict Academy Award winners more accurately than professional entertainment writers for big-city newspapers? As counterintuitive as it seems, the answer is yes to all. Prediction markets really can be utilized in a diverse set of situations.

At Woodbine racetrack in west Toronto, near my home, individual bettors in the pari-mutuel betting line wager on which horse they think will finish first, second, or third in the next race. If a horse goes off at 4:1 odds, bettors are predicting that the horse will win about one-fifth of the time. Odds of 50:1 mean a horse will win, on average, one race in fifty-one. When a 50:1 starter does win, the bettor gets back fifty-one times his original bet: fifty times for choosing the winner, plus a return of the wager.

By betting, each person in the pari-mutuel line shifts the odds toward what they think they should be. If they are confident in their prediction and bet more, they have a greater impact on the odds. When the pari-mutuel windows close sixty seconds before post time, the final odds on each horse represent the collective judgment of those in line.

Some of those in the betting line may be well informed. Most, like me, are pretty naive about what makes one horse run a fraction of a second faster than another. Some bet on the color of the racing silks; others bet only on (or against) female jockeys. Maybe pari-mutuel odds would produce more accurate predictions if we considered only bets placed by the well-informed group. But how would we identify these people in advance? Do the well-informed know who they are? Would they be willing to self-identify? Could we believe them if they did, particularly if they then wanted to sell us their winner-touting advice?

If we can't identify the well-informed, we can determine how good a market result is produced by the mix of well-informed and naive people in the pari-mutual betting line. We need only compare the results from those in line with actual race results over the Woodbine season. We discover that at Woodbine and every other major track, bettors predict almost perfectly how likely a horse is to win. Horses that go off at 3:1 during the Woodbine race season do win one race in four; those at 7:1 win one race in eight.

There is a slight flaw in bettors' predictions, called the *favorite-long-shot* bias; a bit too little is bet on horses that are favored to win, and a tad too much on long shots. There are distorted odds at both extremes. Two dollars bet on a horse with listed odds of more than 99:1 returns, on average, 56 cents. At 30:1, a $2 bet returns on average, 68 cents. At 5:1, it is $1.64. At 2:1, reflecting the favorite bias, it is $1.74. You lose money more slowly betting on favorites. Overbetting on long shots occurs most frequently in the last two races of the day, presumably by bettors trying to recoup their day's losses before heading home.

There are professional horse race handicappers and bookmakers in the United Kingdom and Las Vegas, where such occupations are legal. In the United States, the Professional Handicappers Association has over a hundred members. Some earn a living selling their race predictions on the Internet. These professionals should be experts if anyone is. Some use computer models that factor in the things that are thought to be most important: the previous racing record for each horse, injuries, how long since the horse last raced, the reputation of the jockey, the weight being carried by the horse, the post position, and the condition of the track— soft or hard, wet or dry, dirt or turf. Other racing professionals don't use computer models but rely on experience. They include some of these factors plus how well the horse slept the night before the race and whether it held its head high during the prerace warm-up.

Even factoring in all these considerations, the collectivity of bettors is still a bit more successful at determining odds than professional horse handicappers. The bettors don't outpredict the handicappers by a lot, and not every day, but the market does better over a whole racing season. The most persuasive evidence for the supremacy of the market comes in research by New York University professor Stephen Figlewski. He examined years of results and determined that handicappers were successful in picking the horse that would win 28.7 percent of the time. Bettors, measured by their pari-mutuel betting odds, identified the winning horse 29.4 percent of the time.

Some argue that this result simply reflects that industry professionals with inside information are better able to predict race outcomes. The argument says that these insiders wager more money on each race than naive bettors, and this skews the final odds. The argument is plausible, but seems wrong. The total amount wagered at a track is proportional to the number of people attending. If there are 50 percent more people at

Woodbine on a Saturday than on a Thursday, total wagering on Saturday is about 50 percent higher.

The Figlewski study is supported by another by Michael A. Smith, David Paton, and Leighton Vaughan Williams, who compared bookmaker odds (set early morning on race day) and pari-mutuel odds for the same UK horse races. The study confirmed that pari-mutuel bettor odds are better predictors of race outcomes than the bookmaker equivalents.

The only way to win over a long series of wagers would be to bet not on the horse you think will win, but on the one whose pari-mutuel odds exceed their actual chance of winning. If the odds are 20:1 and you think they should be 10:1, bet. However, pari-mutuel bettors take the "wrong odds" opportunity away by correctly matching odds and outcomes. Plus, of course, the track takes a cut before winners are paid. No one wins over a long series of wagers.

Another comparison comes from betting markets on outcomes of National Football League (NFL) games. Oddsmakers, bookmakers, and the betting public all get involved in those markets. Oddsmakers are the folks who study sports performances and produce the betting odds quoted by media and used by bookmakers. Theirs are the odds you see displayed in sports pages. Oddsmakers only produce odds; they do not take bets. One of the best-known oddsmakers is Las Vegas Sports Consultants, which sells betting odds to Sportsbook, the betting desks in Las Vegas casinos.

Las Vegas Sports Consultants produces a power rating for each NFL team, using a computer program that considers the team's recent performances, the strength of teams it has played, and player injuries. Each team is assigned a new power rating each week. The New York Jets might be assigned a rating of 58 when playing at home, and the Buffalo Bills a 52 when playing a road game. The ratings determine the point spread. The opening betting line for a Buffalo at New York game would be "Jets to win by six points." If you wager on the Jets, the team has to win by seven for you to win. If you wager on the Bills, you win even if they lose by five points or less. Six is a wash, with bets refunded.

Bookmakers are the ones who take bets. The Sportsbook opens with the betting line provided by the oddsmaker. The Sportsbook has to post a plausible number so it does not get clobbered by a wave of early bets on one team. Once bets begin to come in, the betting line changes. The predicted margin of victory point spread shifts to the bookie's estimate of the number required to produce equal betting on each team. This number, which may now be "Jets by 5½," comes from the aggregated wisdom of the thousands of individuals who have wagered on the game—a sports prediction market.

If a Sportsbook moves the betting line to equalize the amount bet on each team, how does it make money? When you wager, you put up $11 to win $10. The $1 difference is the *juice*, or *vigorish*, and the reason Sportsbook and bookies exist. The vigorish compensates for brokering the deal and handling the transfer of funds between the parties. If a Sportsbook can balance bets on each team, the vigorish provides a fat profit margin.

So the betting line you read in the sports page or hear on the radio is not the same one you are quoted at a Sportsbook. Which do you think more accurately predicts actual game-winning point spreads: the odds-maker expert or the bettor-driven sports market? You now think you know the answer, and you are right. The sports market is more accurate than the expert oddsmaker, eight games out of ten. The sports market is also more accurate for all of the so-called *side* or *prop* bets: total points scored, or which team will score the first touchdown.

Because the two predictions are made at different times, the comparison may seem a bit unfair. Between the time the betting line is published in your newspaper and game time, player injuries or inclement weather forecasts may alter the Sportsbook odds. But these balance out. Some players are injured during practice; others recover from prior injuries more quickly than expected. Weather at game time may be better or worse than forecast.

Sports markets not only outpredict experts, in some cases they are close to perfect. Justin Wolfers evaluated the results of 3,791 National Football League games played from 1984 to 2000. He discovered that the Las Vegas betting spread—set by those placing bets on games—predicted 99.7 percent of winning margins. For National Basketball Association games, the betting spread predicted 97.3 percent of winning margins for

9,000 games from 1994 to 2001. NFL and NBA betting markets incorporate all available information such that no expert or group of experts can, over a long period of time, improve on their predictions.

Predicting Academy Awards winners and movie successes provides another market where amateurs and professionals vie for supremacy. Tod and Allison Nielsen, who live in Redmond, Washington, became the subject of a March 2004 article in *Fortune* magazine for incorporating a movie market into their annual black-tie Academy Awards party. Each year the Nielsens ask their sixty party guests to predict winners of the six major Academy Awards prizes:

- Best picture

- Best actor

- Best actress

- Best supporting actor

- Best supporting actress

- Best director

These guests are fairly diverse in age and education. About half work for Microsoft, as Tod did for twelve years. He now comanages VMware, a software company that competes with Microsoft.

For the first seven parties, no guest got all six categories. Each year, the consensus guess beat that of any individual. In 2004, something unusual happened. The consensus media favorites all won. Twelve guests had all six correct, as did the consensus. But the average guest chose only 4.2 winners. The consensus was as good as any individual but better than 80 percent of them.

If black-tie partygoers can pick Academy Awards winners, could MBA students do the same?

Michael Mauboussin is a Wall Street strategist with investment dealer Legg Mason, and author of the 2008 book *More Than You Know: Finding Financial Wisdom in Unconventional Places.* The book was named by

BusinessWeek as one of the top one hundred business books of all time. Mauboussin also teaches an MBA class at Columbia University Business School. Every year since 1993, Mauboussin has given his students a two-sided prediction form a week prior to the Academy Awards ceremony. The front page lists the same six Oscar categories as the Nielsens' party uses. The other side has six more esoteric categories:

- Best adapted screenplay

- Best cinematography

- Best film editing

- Best documentary

- Best art direction

BAKER COLLEGE OF
CLINTON TWP. LIBRARY

A few students may see a lot of movies and know something of these categories. Most students probably see few, given the time demands of their professional program. Each student pays a dollar to take part, winner takes all. The goal is not to support sentimental favorites, but to predict as many Oscar winners as possible and win the pot.

How do these frazzled students perform? Typically the group gets either nine or ten of twelve categories right, with the best individual getting five to seven. The group's consensus vote across twelve categories is always better than the prediction from any individual participant.

The winning student gets a fistful of dollar bills, plus acknowledgment and ego-stroking by the instructor. Mauboussin offers the standard explanation as to why his movie market is so accurate: "All of us walk around with a little information and a substantial error term. When we aggregate our results, the errors tend to cancel each other out and what is distilled is pure information."

Almost every year, the Nielsens' dinner guests and Mauboussin's students are also more accurate than the fan survey results for Academy Awards winners that are published by large-circulation movie magazines. The explanation for that is probably as straightforward as Mauboussin's. If you are interrupted by someone conducting a movie magazine survey, in person or on the phone, you respond as quickly as you can without being rude and then get on with what you were doing. Guests at the dinner party or students in class become engaged in the competitiveness of the process and think much longer about their choices.

This "competitiveness of the market" explanation is reinforced in an experiment by NewsFutures, a public prediction market site that compared prediction of Academy Awards winners by a survey and by a market. The survey achieved 50 percent accuracy, compared with 75 percent for the market. What makes this result intriguing is that the same two hundred people took part in both processes.

Tom Gruca, a marketing professor at the University of Iowa's Tippie College of Business, uses a movie market in his MBA classes. The market is run by the Tippie College, and called the Iowa Electronic Markets (IEM)—and is one of the two or three best-known prediction markets in the world. There is more about the IEM in chapter 4.

Gruca offers a tougher challenge than predicting Academy Awards winners; he asks his students to predict the first four weeks' domestic box-office revenue for a newly released movie. Part of each student's grades reflect how well their investments performed. Each student is provided a $10 trading account. Students can add their own money up to an IEM-imposed limit of $500.

There is not much firsthand information about Hollywood movies available in Iowa. As with Michael Mauboussin's students, Gruca's MBAs probably don't have much spare time for moviegoing. There is a lot of information in the media and on the Web. Each student's task is to determine which sources to rely on.

In 2006, Gruca used the movie *Happy Feet*. This featured singing, dancing, animated penguins. Students started with a little information about how well such films usually do. They could visit the movie's website and download a trailer, ask friends and family for their opinions, and read movie magazine critiques. They knew that the previous year, *The March of the Penguins* (starring real penguins) had performed well at the box office.

Students did not have to be concerned with the moviegoing public's rating of *Happy Feet*'s stars (two animated penguins) or worry about "who is the director." They did have to consider what other movies were opening the same weekend, the box-office record of each A-list human actor involved, the time of year (May is not a good month for openings), and the advance buzz. The consensus student estimate was within 15 percent of the actual box-office revenue.

The IEM's movie markets show how difficult it is to forecast box-office returns. Investors possess few facts, compared to predicting Academy Awards winners. The IEM's four-week box-office predictions are off by an average of 24 percent. That sounds like a rotten result, but other box-office predictions are worse. The IEM is, on average, a more accurate predictor of the first four weeks' box-office receipts than Hollywood publications, professional newsletters, or, I am told, many studio-employed experts. The latter two may, of course, have a bias toward telling studio executives what they want to hear.

Tod and Allison Nielsen's dinner parties and the MBA classes illustrate a couple of the conditions required for good predictions. The predictors are a diverse group, with each person bringing different information to the process. Opinions are independent. Investors can comment on the logic behind their own preference and express their views by groaning or applauding or raising a champagne glass in a toast. But they are not allowed to pressure others to sway their votes.

This "no influencing" condition always strikes people as counterintuitive. You would think that individuals who believe strongly in their Oscar candidates should be allowed to strong-arm others. But when this happens, the argument by the most persuasive or persistent investor may overwhelm those who are less certain. The group prediction then reflects either expert opinion or pooled ignorance.

The "diverse, but no expertise required" idea is also counterintuitive. There is no expectation that the Nielsens' guests or Mauboussin or Gruca's MBA students have seen the movies, or have movie-related expertise (how many guests at any party or students in an MBA class know much about "best cinematography"?). Nor are a large number of participants required for the prediction process. Unlike surveys, where it is preferable to have lots of respondents, a group of forty-five students or sixty partygoers produces good predictions.

There is another market that offers predictions on how well a movie will do. The Hollywood Stock Exchange (HSX) is the largest commercial prediction market in the world. It is run by Cantor Fitzgerald ("Cantor"), a New York–based company involved in investment banking and bond trading. (The name may be familiar from a tragedy; the firm lost many of its employees in the World Trade Center on 9/11.)

Cantor's HSX runs play-money movie markets, which allow studios, actors, directors, and the general public to invest in predicting the future of a motion picture. The HSX exists because, while moviemaking may seem glamorous, it is overall a rotten, unprofitable business. Thousands of movies are produced each year, many financed by eager but naive investors from outside the industry, anxious to have their name appear on screen credits while they mingle with stars.

Less than a hundred of the movies made each year, by major studios or independents, will ever secure national release. At one extreme, a blockbuster but fairly low-budget film, Clint Eastwood's *Gran Torino*, took in $97 million in US box-office receipts in the first two weeks after release and $130 million in the first four. For a successful movie like *Gran Torino*, one-third of total revenue comes from domestic theater box office and two-thirds from foreign releases, television sales, DVDs, branded clothing, and toy deals. For a moderately successful movie release, half of total revenue comes from box office and half from foreign and television sales and DVDs.

At the other extreme—and a more common result—is Sony Pictures' *How Do You Know?*, a comedy featuring Reese Witherspoon as a former softball player. Production cost $120 million, with an additional $18 million spent on marketing. It was introduced in the prime 2010 December pre-Christmas season, was panned by critics, and produced a domestic box office of just $49 million. There were no subsidiary sales of stuffed baseball players, no branded clothing, and not many DVDs.

For both blockbuster films and dogs, 85 percent of domestic box-office revenue comes in the first four weeks after the movie is released. The studio receives about 50 percent of the box-office dollar. A dog will not make it to four weeks; a horrible first-weekend box office means a quick disappearance. Predicted four-week box-office ticket sales are a good proxy for total film revenue, and a matter of intense speculation. A prediction with strong numbers may lead to more marketing and to more theaters showing the movie. Predicted success can become a self-fulfilling prophecy.

Cantor sells the HSX movie market data to financial firms and studios, which combine it with their other information sources to decide what films to invest in, which to release, how much promotion money to throw at a new release, and which scripts to look at in the future.

Why do studios purchase this data when they could simply log on to HSX and get the numbers for free? Cantor owns the demographic information on market investors. Cantor can tell studios the gender and age of those who like and don't like the movie concept and whether supporters are frequent movie attendees, heavy consumers, or early adopters of other entertainment products. Cantor also knows whether support for a movie comes from a relatively small group of avid investors, or if support is more broadly based.

The HSX has 1.8 million registered traders. Each investor starts with 2 million "Hollywood Dollars." About 700,000 people trade at least twice a year. There are 22,000 logins and 40,000 trades on 3,200 films on an average day. A third of investors are from outside the United States. The HSX produces even better predictions than the IEM—about six points better on average.

Some traders are very good. The top trader on HSX is Michael Poster, a thirty-three-year-old corporate and entertainment lawyer from Brooklyn, New York. His portfolio grew from HSX$2 million in 1998 to HSX$1.75 billion in 2011. One of his strategies is to short-sell big movies concepts that he does not think will meet expectations, such as *The Road to Perdition* and *Titan AE*. Poster also invests during the development stage of what he thinks will be blockbuster movies that will later add A-list stars.

HSX sets up a movie market once a project is announced. Investors can then buy, sell, or short-sell stocks. An investor might have decided that the 2010 Harry Potter release was likely to earn $125 million in its first weekend. If the current market price suggests it will make $115 million, he buys at 115. If it does make $125 million, his investment profit is 10. If the box-office take is $103 million, he loses 12.

Short-selling takes place if the investor thinks the market is currently overpriced. Just as on the New York Stock Exchange, the stock is sold first and then bought back later. The investor might first sell at 115, and buy back at 103. If Harry Potter does not meet its $115 million expectations, the investor makes a $12 profit.

If the investor thought the Nicole Kidman movie *Birth* would bomb, she would sell that security at 12½ (which the *Birth* market opened at), on the assumption the movie would take in $12.5 million the first weekend. She would then buy it back at 5 when the actual box office slumps to $5 million.

There is a lot that can be done with movie markets besides predicting winners. The HSX offers executives an opportunity to track the effectiveness of different movie-marketing tactics. From the moment a forthcoming movie is listed on the HSX, studios can use share price movement to test their tactics—release a movie trailer, show a new television commercial, try a buzz-producing Web campaign, or leak details of the movie's plot—then monitor HSX predictions of box-office receipts. A press release that Tom Cruise is dropping out of *Cold Mountain*, or a later one that a new actor will replace him, provides a measure of the box-office value of each. Even monitoring the number of investors in a movie market is informative. Only those comfortable with the concept of the movie will invest in it. Fewer investors equals lower awareness and less comfort.

Harvard marketing professor Anita Elberse has tracked many of these events. She finds that spending a lot of promotional dollars does move first-weekend and four-week box-office prediction markets, but often not enough to cover the additional promotional expense. *Inglourious Basterds*, released in September 2009, cost $65 million to make and budgeted $24 million for prerelease promotion. When the HSX predicted a not-very-good first weekend gross of $27 million, the promotion budget was quickly raised to $35 million. The actual first-weekend box office was $37.6 million. About $5.3 million of the additional box-office money flowed back to the two owners, the Weinstein Company and Universal Pictures—a long way from repaying the additional $11 million in promotion.

Is casting A-list stars worth the cost, given their high salaries? Elberse monitored casting announcements and found that while Tom Hanks, Tom Cruise, or Mel Gibson caused HSX stocks to respond, the predicted box-office increase was often not enough to cover the additional salary cost of the star. She thinks that movie executives pursue stars because they're focusing on revenue rather than profits. Another explanation is that A-list actors attract financing, and their involvement may help in getting domestic and international distribution for the film. Studios could go further and control the experiment by running their own prediction markets and performing experiments. Show a movie advertisement to one set of investors and not to another, then monitor the difference in predicted box-office receipts.

The HSX runs very popular markets each year on who will win Academy Awards. In 2011, the HSX correctly picked seven out of eight top category winners, missing Tom Hooper (*The King's Speech*), who beat David Fincher (*The Social Network*) for best director. In 2010, the HSX also picked seven of eight. In 2009, it was six of eight. The three-year HSX cumulative average is 83 percent. That is a better record than any of the major Hollywood trade papers. It is not quite as good as the Nielsens' dinner guests, who, knowing they will take part in the yearly event, spend more time thinking about competing movies.

In 2010, the Academy Awards changed its nominating and voting procedures to a runoff system. The number of nominees for best picture went from five to ten. More important, the Academy changed the way votes were counted. I wondered what these changes would do to prediction market results.

The old system was *first-past-the-post*—the same as US national elections. There is one round of voting; whoever gets the most votes wins.

This system gives voters an incentive not to vote for their preferred candidate. For example, if in the 2008 presidential election you liked independent candidate Ralph Nader, you might still vote for Barack Obama because you knew Nader could not win. By voting for Obama, you were sure your vote would count. The outcome of first-past-the-post is easier to predict; you only have to estimate first choices.

In 2010, with the Academy's new runoff system, each voter ranked ten candidates for best film, from 1 to 10. The tenth-ranked movie was dropped from consideration, votes were recounted, the ninth-ranked was dropped, and so on. In such a system, your vote will always count, so you have an incentive to vote for the film you really prefer.

Could prediction markets still pick winners from this more complex runoff system? Markets chose *The Hurt Locker* over *Avatar* for best picture (the closest race); Sandra Bullock for best actress; Jeff Bridges for best actor; Mo'Nique for best supporting actress; Christoph Waltz as best supporting actor; and Kathryn Bigelow (*The Hurt Locker*) to beat her ex-husband James Cameron (*Avatar*) for best director (also a very close call). Markets were right on all of these Oscars. Were these results just derivative, with investors arbitraging information from movie column writers? Every major media predictor in Los Angeles got at least one category wrong; most missed two or three.

The HSX offers an interesting insight on what movie markets think about economics topics. In 2007, there was an announcement that Alex Gibney, who later won a 2008 Academy Award for the documentary *Taxi to the Dark Side*, planned to make a documentary film based on the 2005 trade book *Freakonomics* by Steven Levitt and Stephen Dubner. This is one of the best-selling economics books of all time, with 4 million copies in print.

The HSX stock opened with a predicted four-week box office of $7 million. Investors immediately sold *Freakonomics* short, and the price started falling in a manner reminiscent of Enron. In six months, it dropped 85 percent, to about $1 million. Three months later it was at $800,000. There are several possible explanations for this slump, including the general lack of publicity after the project was announced. The most likely one is lack of enthusiasm. The longer investors thought about how excited moviegoers would be about seeing a movie on economics—even on topics as entertaining as those in *Freakonomics*—the more appealing it was to short-sell.

Freakonomics! The Movie was released in October 2010 with few screens, modest reviews, a very brief run, and an $840,000 domestic box office. The market was right. Your chance of seeing the MGM lion roar to open the movie version of *Oracles* is slim.

4

Election Markets

*There are lots of reasons to lie to pollsters, but none to make a
money-losing bet.*

—Tim Harford, economist

*Someone should do a study on how all the American liberals are
obsessively logging in to Intrade to view their electoral prediction
map. Doctors are going to start prescribing it in place of Xanax,
for anxiety.*

—Chad Rigetti, VP of Intrade, quoting a friend during the 2008
presidential election

IF MARKETS CAN predict movie success, can they predict political success? Can they predict not only the next American president, but also
the junior senator from Nebraska and what party will control Congress
after the next election?

Election markets have a very long history. One of the first involved the
selection of new cardinals in the Catholic Church. Historians Paul Rhode
and Koleman Strumpf report that odds on papal succession appeared
as early as 1503, when such wagering was already referred to as "an old
practice." The attendants to cardinals in conclave were known to partner
with bettors. In 1591, Pope Gregory XIV banned "on pain of excommu-

nication," all betting on the election of a new pope, the selection of new cardinals, or the length of a papacy.

A public betting market on presidential elections existed in the United States from 1880 until World War II. There were times in the early twentieth century when betting volume on political outcomes at the New York Curb Exchange (the precursor of the New York Stock Exchange) exceeded the dollar value of trading in bonds and stocks. The odds that resulted from this activity were both public and accurate. In October 1904, the *New York Times* quoted financier Andrew Carnegie's press conference declaration: "From what I see of the betting . . . I do not think Mr. Roosevelt will need my vote . . . I am sure of his election."

Some who could not afford large stakes backed their election beliefs with creative wagers involving public humiliation for the loser. A common side bet required the loser not only to hand over cash but to use a toothpick to roll a peanut down the town's main street. Or the losing bettor paid up by eating crow—literally eating the bird—in public. Twenty-first-century election markets treat failed investors more gently.

Scientific forecasting of US presidential elections began in the mid 1930s with two polling organizations; one run by George Gallup, the second by Elmo Roper. Polls produced *insiders*—those who had access to polling results before they were made public. Knowing that these insiders existed deterred some bettors from participating in election markets. Presidential betting markets had disappeared by the beginning of World War II.

Today, the IEM, a prediction market run by a business school in Iowa City, and Intrade, an offshore prediction market in Ireland, each produce better predictions on presidential and other US elections than political pollsters. Market results improve on "the best political commentators on television," CNN's hourly-repeated 2008 election-reporting tagline. Election prediction markets in 2008 called the presidential outcome with greater accuracy than either polls or television pundits, just as markets had in previous elections.

To understand why, compare election markets with Gallop Poll surveys. Pollsters try to question a randomly selected sample of people, but some can't be located, others refuse to take part, and still others provide the quickest possible answer to get rid of the pollster. There is no information about whether a respondent really intends to vote—most, if asked, say they will. Without knowing this intention, pollsters give equal weight to those who say they prefer Democrats but may not vote and those who say they prefer Republicans and do vote. Those over forty-five who favor Republicans have a likelihood of voting that starts at 60 percent and rises with age. Twenty- to thirty-year-olds who favor Democrats have a less-than-40-percent likelihood of voting. That latter figure rose a bit with Barack Obama's 2008 presidential campaign, but still did not exceed 45 percent in any state.

By contrast, election market investors self-select. They put their own money and egos on the line. The more confident they are, the more money they invest. Those who make good political predictions make money. Those who think they can make good predictions but fail, lose money and drop out. Those who are not interested or see themselves as having little insight do not take part.

The modern history of US election markets began in March 1988, in Iowa City, Iowa. As the story is told, three economists from the University of Iowa were having an after-class beer at an Iowa City pizza place and sports bar called the Airliner and discussing how inaccurate political polls sometimes were. The previous day had seen a surprise win in the Michigan Democratic presidential primary by civil rights activist Jesse Jackson. Reverend Jackson defeated Michael Dukakis, when every poll predicted Jackson would receive only 5 to 10 percent of the vote.

George Neumann, Robert Forsythe, and Forrest Nelson were amazed that no pollster or political commentator had predicted a Jackson win. The three shared an interest in experimental economics, in which economic theory is tested by examining group behavior. Nelson proposed, half in jest, that they should start a market to predict the coming presidential election. They came up with several alternative proposals, diagrammed on a succession of paper napkins.

There were hidden booby traps in setting up an election market within a state university. Using Iowa undergraduate students to predict national behavior was counterintuitive to everybody. An election market using real money appeared, at first glance, to have a lot of similarities to an organized gambling ring. So Neumann, Forsythe, and Nelson sought cover from the dean of the business school and the head of the economics department. The dean, a fan of experimental economics, thought the proposal sounded great. The head of economics is said to have described it as stupid. The three decided that one favorable vote out of two constituted a green light.

The election market initiative set up shop in what is now the Tippie School of Business. The three researchers addressed the gambling concern by getting the Iowa attorney general to agree that it was actually a kind of office betting pool, thus legal under Iowa law.

And so on June 1, 1988, the Iowa Political Stock Market was born; the formal name was later changed to the Iowa Electronic Markets (IEM). The original market design was copied from the Iowa pork bellies market. Instead of pigs, the 1988 market traded presidential election contracts on George H. W. Bush (Republican), Michael Dukakis (Democrat), Ron Paul (Libertarian), and Lenora Fulani (New Alliance). Paul ended up with one-half of 1 percent of the final vote in 1988, and resurfaced as a presidential candidate in 2008. Fulani ended up with one-fifth of 1 percent, and did not run again. The market was pre-Internet, with all transactions on paper.

The first investments on the IEM were on what would later be called a *vote share market*—a share on a candidate paid off based on that candidate's final vote percentage. An investor bought a Dukakis security at 43 cents, corresponding to the candidate's then perceived share of the market. If Dukakis received 46 percent of the vote on Election Day, the investor made a three-cent profit—even though Dukakis lost the election.

Later, the IEM offered winner-take-all contracts. In 2008, you could buy an Obama security at the current price, say 49 cents, and receive $1 if the candidate won and nothing if he lost. The trader who purchased at 49 cents could also choose to sell her Obama security before the election, say at 56 cents, earning a 7-cent profit.

Over several elections, the vote share market has provided slightly more accurate predictions than the winner-take-all markets, probably because more thought goes to predicting vote share than to predicting a winner.

That first 1988 Iowa market attracted eight hundred investors and a dollar volume of $8,100. The participants were, as you might guess, young (most under twenty-three), white, male, from a rural background, and mostly (80 percent) from Iowa. The group could not have been further from representing a cross-section of American society.

The evening of Election Day 1988 was crunch time for the Iowa market. Would the final price for Bush and Dukakis shares predict the actual vote split for the candidates as accurately as the well-financed Gallup, Harris, and CBS/New York Times polls? All three correctly predicted Bush would win. The average error in the three was 1.9 percent; the Iowa Political Stock Market predicted a Bush win with an error of one-tenth of 1 percent. Neumann and his colleagues were on to something.

For the 1992 presidential campaign, the IEM was opened up to investors around the world. It could no longer be presented as an office betting pool, particularly because it was now accepting individual investments up to $500. University officials were getting edgy about the legality and morality of what was taking place in a back room at the business school.

After some scrambling, the IEM found a semipermanent solution to the gambling concern in 1993 by securing a so-called "no-action" letter from Andrea M. Corcoran, director of the US Commodity Futures Trading Commission's Trading and Markets Division. The letter promised that the business school would not be prosecuted by the Commission as long as the IEM was used for academic purposes, did not advertise, and did not allow the administrators to profit from it—although the business school could (and did). While the risk of prosecution under state gambling statutes was not entirely eliminated, the academics who ran the IEM now thought they could persuade a court that a government agency had categorized their election market as a commodity exchange.

For the five presidential races from 1988 to 2004, there were 964 polls. The IEM was more accurate than the polls 74 percent of the time. In the week before each of the four presidential elections from 1988 to 2000, the

Iowa election markets showed an average error of 1.4 percent, compared to 2.1 percent for the Gallup Poll.

In 2004, the IEM consistently showed George W. Bush ahead. For most of the month prior to the election, various polls indicated Democrat John Kerry with a lead of as much as seven percentage points. The evening before the election the IEM showed Bush with 50.45 percent of the vote and Kerry with 49.55 percent. The actual count was 51.56 percent for Bush, 48.44 percent for Kerry.

The IEM does fall prey to some of the same glitches that occur in other prediction markets and polls. On Election Day, investors rely too heavily on information that comes out at the last minute, or during the first hours of voting—which is why the best measure of accuracy is market results the evening before the election. The other failure occurs when election markets deal with events that are highly unlikely to occur—a "political long-shot bias." Election traders, like racetrack bettors, place too much weight on an underdog victory. When racetrack markets get below a 10 percent chance of winning, horses rarely win. Neither do Lenora Fulani or Ralph Nader.

Beginning with the 2004 presidential election market, television and print journalists began citing IEM results alongside polling results as a measure of how political races were going. In a couple of cases, they cited IEM results without bothering with polls.

The folks who were investing in the IEM were (and are) still very far from being representative of the whole population. The most recent survey showed traders as 90 percent male, 90 percent white, 89 percent in college or with college degrees, 70 percent registered Republicans, and 60 percent from households with incomes greater than $75,000. Most had grown up in Iowa. Ninety-five percent reported that they planned to vote. Investors also self-reported a much higher than average confidence in their own political insights. No student in a college statistics course would risk a failing grade by suggesting this group as a good sample for any experimental purpose whatsoever.

Critics correctly point out that it is a bit misleading to compare election market results with poll results. The two are inherently different creatures. A poll asks whom you would vote for if the election were held that day. The IEM and other markets ask whom you think will win on the actual Election Day. In 2004, you may have preferred John Kerry over George W. Bush, and if asked by a pollster, you might have declared that your candidate was sure to win. But when it came to investing in an election market, you probably bought the George W. Bush security. In 2004, 68 percent of self-reported Democrats taking part in the IEM said they would vote for Kerry. At least half of those appear to have invested in Bush.

Some investors take part in the IEM through robot-automated traders, "bots" that buy or sell contracts when prices get lower or higher than the trader thinks is justified, or when prices are lower on one election market than on another. These are the same programs used to execute trades on major stock exchanges. About one-fifth of IEM trades are now carried out by bots.

The existence of bots allows investors to trade no matter what the time; there is a bot willing to buy from or sell to the trader who logs on at 3 a.m. Bot trades also keep each market in balance by offsetting large trades that otherwise would move prices too much.

The 2008 US presidential election was boring whether you followed election markets or polls. For the last six weeks of the campaign, every market and poll showed Barack Obama as the winner. But markets did produce interesting insights into the political process. Early IEM and Intrade polls showed the importance national voters attached to the results of the January 3 Iowa caucus. Before this was held, Barack Obama was a 32 percent favorite to win the Democratic nomination. After winning Iowa—a state with a population (3.1 million) about equal to that of the San Francisco Bay area—Obama's numbers moved to 64 percent. Hillary Clinton dropped to a distant second, and John Edwards, in spite of finishing second in Iowa, dropped from 6 to 2 percent.

Mike Huckabee's surprise win in the Iowa Republican caucus raised his standing only a little, but former Massachusetts governor Mitt Romney's poor showing dropped him from 25 to 12 percent in the IEM and catapulted John McCain to a lead he never relinquished. Rudy Giuliani, who did not campaign in Iowa, finished badly in the caucus vote there, dropped dramatically in the IEM, and never recovered. At the time, these changes in market probabilities were viewed as a short-term reaction. The market was expected to return in a couple of days to where it had been prior to the Iowa caucus. It never happened.

The 2008 vice presidential selection process showed how well election markets can function even when information is widely dispersed. A week before Obama's naming of a vice presidential nominee, Evan Bayh was ranked as the Democratic frontrunner, with Tim Kaine a strong second. Joe Biden was a weak third, with about 7 percent support, and Kansas governor Kathleen Sebelius a close fourth. As more information about each of these candidates emerged, Biden's security moved into first place—this at a time when no CNN political commentator rated him in the top four. A few hours before Biden was named, he was trading at 80 percent to be the nominee.

No election market, poll, or CNN pundit foresaw that McCain would name Alaska governor Sarah Palin as his running mate. Election markets alternated between Minnesota governor Tim Pawlenty and Mitt Romney as the favorite. Tom Ridge, the former director of Homeland Security, was third, and Palin a weak fourth. Palin was at no point prior to announcement day ever mentioned on CNN as a possible nominee.

A day before the announcement, a blogger with a source at the Anchorage airport reported that Palin and her family had chartered a flight to Ohio, which would arrive just before McCain's nominee-announcement press conference. Intrade created a Palin security, other investors sought information and jumped in, and three hours before she was first mentioned on CNN, her Intrade contract reflected an 82 percent chance of her being chosen.

Intrade created a contract to measure the success of the October 2 vice presidential debate. If Obama's share price improved after the debate— meaning that McCain's went down—the market was saying that Biden had won the debate, and vice versa. It was possible to watch the presidential contracts move in real time, debating point by debating point. During the Palin presentation, McCain prices moved up just under two points, suggesting Palin had surpassed viewers' expectations. During the Biden presentation, Obama prices moved up about half a point.

This Intrade market illustrated the degree to which political partisans show a "home-team" bias when estimating the likelihood that their candidate will win—and how markets overcome this. Of Republicans who watched the televised vice presidential debate, 65 percent told pollsters that Sarah Palin had won; 61 percent of Democrats who watched said Joe Biden had won. Investors settled at 52–48 in favor of Palin. Those investing either had second thoughts, or responded differently when asked to put up money. Each invested at a 13 percent lower probability than they had stated to pollsters.

The last six months of the 2008 presidential race paralleled the implosion of the world's capital markets. In the past, market shifts had been a good predictor of election outcomes. In twenty presidential elections from 1928 to 2004, the market had risen in the three months prior to the vote on fourteen occasions and dropped on six. Of the fourteen ups, the candidate of the party in power was reelected eleven times. Of the six downs, the opposition party won five times. Stock market movement as a predictor had an 80 percent success rate.

IEM and Intrade markets showed McCain and Obama running neck and neck until the stock market began to decline in May and June. The S&P 500 bottomed out on July 15, 2008, and so did McCain shares. The stock market rallied a bit thereafter, as did McCain shares. Both peaked in September. In mid-October, winner-take-all markets said McCain had a 47 percent chance of winning the White House. Two days before the election, that figure had dropped to 17 percent, tracking the failure of Lehman Brothers and the gloomy financial headlines.

What can prediction markets tell us about the conventional belief that the economy drives presidential fortunes? Everyone who follows politics remembers James Carville's dismissive comment from the 1992 election, "It's the economy, stupid." The 2008 prediction markets seem to support that idea. However, a parallel movement of the stock market and presidential fortunes does not prove causation. It can equally be argued that a poor economy brings down both stocks and the incumbent party.

Perhaps Wall Street investors sold stocks as Obama's chances of winning increased; Senator Obama was seen by some as a closet socialist whose policies would handicap American business. Or perhaps markets feared the prospect of Democrats controlling both houses of Congress plus the presidency, allowing populist economics to flourish.

John Authers, the investment editor of London's *Financial Times*, provides another explanation. He believes that voters' confidence in the future is tied to stock prices because pensions are largely invested in stocks. When voters see themselves as worse off, they are more willing to try the candidate who promises change. So choose your theory. I'm with Bill Clinton: "It's the economy."

How else could election markets be used? Consider one application that is analogous to contracts dealing with the Iraq invasion and the price of oil. During the 2008 election campaign, skyrocketing oil prices were seen by voters as the most visible indicator of bad economic management by then-President George W. Bush. So which presidential candidate was seen as best able to constrain oil prices?

Assume that in August 2008, with oil prices at $145 a barrel, the IEM or Intrade had offered two contracts. The first would pay $100 if Obama won the election and crude prices fell below $90 a barrel by May 1, 2009. If Obama lost, the contract would be void and the investor would get his money back. The second contract would pay $100 if McCain won and crude prices fell below $90 by the same date. Should McCain lose, his contract would be void and the investor repaid.

The difference between the asking price for each of the two contracts is one measure of the market's expectation of whether Obama or McCain would do a better job with the economy. The spread between the two prices, and movements in the price levels, each provide a measure of the change in voter expectations. The caveat, again, is that these paired markets may reveal correlation rather than causation. Voters may be more willing to cast ballots for Obama if they believe that oil prices will fall to more normal levels within the next few months.

We know now that a $90 price would have been a very modest target; oil prices had fallen below $40 by the end of December. But in August 2008, a $90 price seemed wildly optimistic.

A conditional prediction market with the same structure was used in the 2004 presidential election to assess the link between the presidential race and the war against terrorism. Justin Wolfers and Eric Zitzewitz ran a market on Irish prediction market site TradeSports.com, linking the reelection of George W. Bush and the capture of Osama bin Laden. The market suggested a 91 percent probability of Bush being reelected if Osama were caught, and a 67 percent chance if not.

A second set of markets suggested that investors thought the desirability of apprehending Osama just before the November election was not lost on the Bush administration. Markets predicted a 6 percent chance of a September capture and 8 percent in October, but a 4 percent chance in each of November and December.

The fact that there are so many election markets dealing with the same event might seem to cast doubt on the finding that markets beat polls. Be selective about the choice of market and poll to compare, and you can state that markets win, right?

The answer is no. With multiple election markets offering the same contracts, marginal traders sell in more expensive candidate markets and buy in the less expensive, causing all markets to offer pretty much the same price. This is the same process that produces identical prices for the euro against the dollar in London, New York, Dubai, and Hong Kong.

5

Estimation Markets

Rail travel at high speed is not possible, because passengers, unable to breathe, would die of asphyxia.

> —Dr. Dionysus Larder, professor of philosophy and astronomy,
> University College London, 1851

The atom bomb will never go off—and I speak as an expert in explosives.

> —US Admiral William Leahy, 1945

PREDICTION MARKETS offer a probability that an event will take place. That probability changes over time as circumstances change; for example, as a presidential election campaign rolls out. What is the chance of Joe Biden being replaced as the vice presidential nominee?

There is another set of markets, where each outcome has a determinably correct answer, one that does not change over time. The challenge for an investor in these markets is to identify the right answer. There are various names for these—let's call them *estimation markets*. Which US president once appeared on the television show *Laugh-In*? What will be the temperature at noon next Tuesday? How many jellybeans are there in an apothecary jar? Estimation markets tell us a lot about how prediction markets work.

A fun question is, "How many windows are there on a London double-decker bus?" Ask one person chosen at random to estimate and you will probably not get an accurate answer. Ask three people and you will get three different answers.

Then ask each person in a room of fifty to estimate. Those with some knowledge—who may have visited London and seen or ridden on a double-decker or at least have a visual image of the bus from photos—will take part. Those who can't even visualize the bus probably will not. The average estimate of all those who take part will produce a pretty accurate answer, perhaps better than any individual prediction within the group. (The answer is not, as you might assume, an even number. The traditional red Routemaster double-decker has twenty-three windows: ten on each side, one at the front, and two at the rear. The lengthened RML Routemaster, which fewer in the crowd will be familiar with, has 27 windows: 12 on each side, one front, two rear.)

Jack Treynor teaches finance at Yale's School of Management. To illustrate the way individual investors produce a trading price for a NASDAQ stock, he has class members guess the number of jellybeans in a jar. The jar contains 850 jellybeans. The average guess is within 25 jellybeans, or 3 percent, of the correct answer.

Many college instructors use jellybean guessing to illustrate different economic ideas. Finance students at the Wharton School at the University of Pennsylvania do a jellybean experiment to estimate future stock market levels, and take the exercise so seriously that some record their competitive rank on their résumés, anticipating an employment-related reward.

I ask my MBA students to estimate the number of jellybeans in an old-fashioned bell-shaped apothecary jar as an introduction to the concept of a prediction market and the role of experts. Even though none of my students knows much about the volume of a tapered cylinder, or the density of settled jellybeans, the collective estimate from a group of forty students is always within a few percentage points of being correct. As with Treynor's classes, the group estimate is always closer than all but one or two of the individual estimates, sometimes closer than any individual guess. The range of individual estimates is all over the place, from 60 percent too low to 50 percent too high.

If I ran the experiment a number of times with the same class but different-sized jars and beans, one or two people might beat the collective estimate each time. But I suspect it would be different students for each trial.

After the experiment I ask the class why this is happening. A student will offer an explanation along the lines of: "All that happens is that there are a few people with some expertise who make an informed guess. There are a lot of us with no particular expertise, who guess too high or too low. The highs and lows average out, leaving the expert guesses. You could have done as well by simply asking the experts in the class."

"OK," I respond. "That sounds logical. Now someone please tell me who the jellybean experts in the class are. We'll redo the experiment and just ask them." Everyone grins a little self-consciously, but no one will hazard a nomination. So much for identifying experts.

"Fair enough," I say. "Let's have the experts self-identify. All those who are expert in jellybean guessing, raise your hand." Usually no one does. Occasionally one overly confident student volunteers, then one or two others might follow. They usually claim expertise based on backgrounds in mathematics or engineering.

The same question arises as with horse betting touts: are the self-identified experts any better than those who don't consider themselves expert? Remember, with jellybean guessing, I know the estimates submitted by each student a few minutes earlier. The names were included with the estimate slips, so I would know who wins the prize. Does one of the self-identified experts have the best individual estimate? Almost never. The experience of everyone who has done this experiment is that the group can't identify experts, and experts can't self-identify.

After competing for a jellybean prize that no one cares much about (the winner always shares with the class during the next break), I ask if anyone wants to put up $5 and take part in a second round of estimation. The winner of the second round gets the money.

About half of the class will stay in. Then a strange thing happens. The second round, with about $100 at stake, produces an average guess closer to the actual number of jellybeans than did the first. Students visibly take more time and put more thought into their second-round prediction. They still have the same basic information: a rough sense of how many jellybeans might fit the bottom layer of the tapered cylinder, a guess as to how many beans high the cylinder is, and a guess as to how much to discount for the taper. They multiply, add a few percent for compression, and record their guess.

There are now fewer extreme estimates; the range narrows from 60 percent too low and 50 percent too high, to half that in each direction. Those who drop out are not deterred by the $5 buy-in; they are students who know they have little knowledge to bring to this prediction exercise. The average first-round estimate of the dropouts had three times the error percentage of those who stayed in for the second round.

To put the $5 buy-in ante in context, the participants are graduate students with a median age of twenty-nine; many are part-time students with full-time jobs. After class, they will spend that much or more on a Starbucks coffee and danish, or a beer. The $5 stake does not seem to be a deterrent. The results of the $5 round suggest that it may not always be correct to assume that play money or a small prize will produce the same results as a more substantial real-money reward. In this experiment at least, cash trumps jellybeans.

I have on several occasions suggested a third prediction round. This time there would be a $20 buy-in, to see if a higher incentive produces still better predictions. But at $20, only three or four people offer to stay in. The result would be inconclusive, so I cancel this round.

The classic group-estimate story involves Francis Galton and a soon-to-be-slaughtered ox. Galton was a famous nineteenth-century British mathematician and social commentator, a cousin to Charles Darwin, and the originator of the now widely used technique of statistical regression. (His other contributions include the first classification system for fingerprints, the first newspaper weather map, and a detailed published account of how to brew the perfect cup of tea.)

Galton also founded the science of eugenics; the word comes from the Greek *eugenes,* meaning "good heredity." He developed eugenics as part of his argument for the selective breeding of humans of good health and high intelligence.

In 1906, Galton attended the West of England Fat Stock and Poultry Exhibition in the town of Plymouth and watched fairgoers purchasing sixpenny raffle tickets. Each ticket entitled the bearer to one guess of the dressed weight of the ox. The entrant who guessed closest to the correct weight took home the dressed carcass. Galton thought the raffle device was brilliant. Fairgoers entertained themselves, and the ox-owner took in more money selling prediction opportunities than he ever could by selling ox meat.

After the raffle, and on a whim, Galton asked for the nonwinning tickets with weight estimates. He took the tickets home to check the quality of the estimates. Given his cynical view on the intelligence of the average human, he thought they would be pretty bad. A few guesses might be decent; in the crowd there were stockmen and butchers. Most predictions would reflect little knowledge, although a few would be close because of sheer luck. Maybe the winner of the ox carcass, a dry-goods shopkeeper, was one of the lucky ones.

The median of the 787 estimates that Galton could decipher was 1,189 pounds. The average estimate was 1,197 pounds. The actual dressed weight of the ox was 1,198 pounds. The shopkeeper's winning prediction was 1,170 pounds. No single guess was as close as that represented by the crowd's median or mean. Galton had the sudden insight that a group might produce better estimates than any individual, even if that group was composed of only a few people who knew a lot about the subject, plus many who knew little.

Galton later used his "crowds are actually clever" conclusion to reverse his negative perception of the undereducated, less-prosperous common man. He now argued that a democracy that gave everyone the vote would produce a better result than a system where only the educated or the wealthy could vote. His "everyone must take part" idea was the origin of *vox populi*—the "voice of the people."

A ten-year research project by Scott E. Page, a Caltech professor, provides more recent evidence of how diversity beats ability. The value of diversity caught Page's interest in 1995 when he was running a computer simulation of how subjects in his lab experiments interacted to solve problems. One program represented the behavior of those who held graduate degrees; the second mimicked a group of individuals with varied backgrounds and experience. The second group composition was like choosing decision makers by selecting only those born on the first day of a month.

When he ran the program, Page found the diverse group made better choices than the graduate-degree holders—not on straightforward problems like the most efficient way to fly an aircraft or change a light bulb, but on complex problems where there are no obvious rules to be applied. Page rewrote the program and tried different approaches. He changed how the decision makers could interact. He changed how the result was judged. Each time the diverse group, the first-of-monthers, were better at solving problems.

The results of Page's research are set out in his 2007 book, *The Difference,* in which he explains that people of high ability generally have similar perspectives and apply the same problem-solving techniques. These experts are better than the diverse group only for problems requiring narrowly focused ability. The diverse group would not be very good at designing a railroad bridge. They would bring a more diverse set of tools, and would be better at predicting how many people would choose to take a train over a plane between the two now-connected cities. Page says, "This theorem is no mere metaphor or cute empirical anecdote that may or may not be true ten years from now. It is a logical truth."

What Page is talking about is not gender, age, race, and religion, which constitute social identity diversity. What he finds important is *cognitive* diversity, which includes experience, background, and education. Social identity diversity is about what individuals bring to the discussion and how they get along. Cognitive diversity is about how people think, about their approaches to solving a problem like the weight of an ox. Social identity diversity sometimes matches up well with cognitive diversity, but they are not the same thing.

Lack of diversity in a group can produce worse decisions. In his 2008 book *Going to Extremes*, Cass Sunstein, then a professor at Harvard Law School, says people with the same views seek others with similar beliefs. The grouping causes their views to grow more extreme. Sunstein conducted an experiment where he separated politicians into two groups, liberal Democrats and conservative Republicans. He had them deliberate on controversial issues such as same-sex marriage. In interviews conducted before the experiment, individual members expressed their position on each issue. Without diversity, each group later reached consensus on a more radical outcome than had the average of its members.

Sunstein claims that the polarization of nondiverse groups helps explain Islamic terrorism, the Enron collapse, and many of the failures during the presidency of George W. Bush, whose administration, he says, encouraged group polarization.

The point of Page and Sunstein's work—and that of everyone who emphasizes the importance of diversity in a market—is that markets can be rational, even when some of the people investing in them are not. With investor diversity, errors cancel out and markets arrive at appropriate estimates, as happened with Galton's fairgoers and my MBA students. The issue turns out to be not whether investors are irrational or uninformed, but whether they are irrational or uninformed in the same way. If they are different, errors cancel and the dynamic of the wise collective rules. Page's work provides a theoretical underpinning to much of the anecdotal evidence of how prediction markets work, and why they so often outperform experts.

The long-running television show *Who Wants to Be a Millionaire* originated in the United Kingdom in 1998. It has since been produced in local editions in eighty-two countries, including Russia, Macedonia, Japan, Vietnam, and Afghanistan. The English title of the show comes from a Cole Porter song in the 1956 movie *High Society*. The lyrics are actually "Who wants to be a millionaire? I don't, 'cause all I want is you!"

Who Wants to Be a Millionaire demonstrates how groups of diverse people surpass experts in providing correct answers. In the television show, contestants answer a series of twelve to fifteen increasingly difficult questions. Cash awards start low and become larger with each winning round until the final-round prize is 1 million of the currency of the country in which the show takes place. Each question is multiple-choice, with four possible answers. A contestant who is unsure of an answer can either take the money already won and go home, or ask to use a lifeline.

There are three kinds of lifelines. In one, the show's computer randomly eliminates two of four possible answers. A second lifeline involves polling the studio audience. In this ask-the-audience option, individuals indicate their preferred answer through an A-B-C-D response button at their seats. The results are displayed on the screen for the contestant, host, and audience to see. In a variant of this lifeline, users of AOL Instant Messenger can also take part. The television studio screen shows the audience's response, then the AOL users' response.

In the third option, the contestant can telephone a friend or relative, a previous contestant, or any smart person who is willing to stand by. These supports are chosen because they have expertise in question areas where the contestant thinks himself to be weak.

Contrary to what the show's producers expected, in every national version of *Millionaire* but two, the ask-the-audience option produces far more correct answers than ask-the-expert. In all of these shows, audience members are a random, diverse group: those who appear at the front of the line on the day of the taping. Their only common characteristic may be that they had nothing more engrossing to do on a weekday afternoon.

In the US edition of the program, audiences are right 92 percent of the time and expert friends 65 percent. In the UK edition, it is 87 percent audience, 55 percent experts; in the German edition, it is 90 percent and 58 percent. One explanation is that easier, pop-culture questions get referred to the audience and more difficult technical questions are referred to friends. But is it plausible that this also happens in Japan and Afghanistan? A more likely answer is that the result mimics the jellybean example. If a small number of individuals in the audience know the right answer, and others guess more or less randomly, the group prediction will be accurate.

A $1 million question posed by host Regis Philbin was mentioned at the beginning of this chapter: "Which US president appeared on the television series *Laugh-In*?" Possible answers were Lyndon Johnson, Richard Nixon, Jimmy Carter, and Gerald Ford. Let's say only 12 percent of the audience—18 of 150 people—actually saw and remembered that episode of *Laugh-In* from viewing the broadcast or a rerun. That leaves 88 percent of the audience who were too young, or had not read about it. They lack any insight, but most would still vote.

About 22 percent will randomly choose each of the four options. The audience-choice board would show 34 percent (12 percent + 22 percent) choosing the correct answer, Richard Nixon. Then 22 percent would choose each of Presidents Johnson, Carter, and Ford. Note that we could add more people who lack insight without changing the result. Add fifty more uninformed audience members. While the percentage favoring Nixon will decline, he will still be selected. A very small percentage of the group can produce a correct answer. As long as the remaining investors are diverse and their predictions are random, the collective prediction will be right.

Princeton politics professor Adam Meirowitz has suggested how a true prediction market could be used in *Millionaire*. Imagine if Regis Philbin offered as the million-dollar question a problem for which only a well-trained mathematician could be certain of getting right. Only if the contestant knew and called one of these mathematicians (assuming she was not one), would she get the right answer. If she polled the audience, even if the diverse audience contained five people with the right training, the randomness from the nonmathematicians might overwhelm the five knowledgeable members. The audience poll might be correct, but not by much and not always.

However, if instead of polling the audience, the contestant were offered a different lifeline—create a prediction market for the audience and watch the trading—the correct result would emerge. Those trained in mathematics would continue to invest until the market price reflected their subjective confidence about the right answer. Unfortunately, this would make for less-than-gripping television.

The *Millionaire* market idea works only if there is no limit on the amount an individual can invest. If there is an investment cap and the knowledgeable mathematicians reach it, they may not be able to move the overall result far enough toward the correct answer. With a small cap and an audience where many members know the right answer, the market will select accurately. The two variables are the number of informed audience members and the size of the investment cap. If the prediction market gets one of those right, the contestant gets the correct answer and wins the million.

There were two countries where the audience does not produce more accurate answers—France and Russia. In *Qui Veut Gagner Des Millions*, the French edition of *Millionaire*, audiences seem to intentionally choose the wrong answer when polled on earlier, low-value questions—for example, "What three colors are in the French flag?" (blue, white, and red). Apparently French audiences think it unfair that anyone too ignorant to answer a simple question should benefit from the audience's wisdom. On later, difficult questions, a French audience does try to provide the correct answer.

In *Миллионер*, the Russian edition of the program, audiences provide incorrect answers to mislead contestants on both simple and difficult questions, apparently because of a residual cultural acceptance of the core communist teaching that it is unfair for anyone to get rich from the knowledge of the collective.

The moral seems to be that if you are going to rely on a market, make sure the participants want you to find the right answer.

What other kinds of estimation market produce unexpected results? One is a weather market. My untrained students can predict medium-term weather much as they predict jellybean numbers. I ask a class of MBA students to forecast the temperature at noon at Toronto International Airport, five days from the day of the class. I don't ask for the next-day temperature because too many have heard a local forecast on their car radio, and will repeat that number.

The average of the student temperature estimates for noon five days hence will be more accurate than four-fifths of the individual estimates. The average prediction will also be more accurate than the five-day advance forecast provided by the Toronto Weather Service, two times in three.

The result is not that surprising, even though no student has specialized knowledge or thinks much about the weather five days in advance. Each participant knows something about today's temperature, seasonal trends, and whether the past few days have been particularly warm or cool. The weather example is like estimating the weight of an ox or the number of jellybeans. Each estimate reflects some knowledge, some randomness, and some bias. Randomness and bias cancel out, and knowledge remains.

The temperature-predicting success is due in part to my choice of a five-day period. Professional weather forecasters are quite accurate three days out but have lower accuracy for days four, five, and beyond. Because of movement of the jet stream, low-pressure cells, and other factors, their seven-day forecast is not much more than talented guesswork.

Ask my students to predict rainfall five days hence and they flounder. Predicting rainfall five days out is an example of a market with garbage-in information, garbage-out results. Professional forecasters provide excellent seventy-two-hour rainfall forecasts. For all the times they say "There is a 30 percent chance of rain tomorrow," it will indeed rain the next day about 30 percent of the time—exactly what "30 percent chance" means. Beyond seventy-two hours, their rainfall forecasts also deteriorate to talented guesswork.

6

What Can Prediction Markets Replace?

If you had to identify, in one word, the reason why the human race has not achieved, and never will achieve, its full potential, that word would be "meetings."

   —Dave Barry, humorist

In any great organization it is far, far safer to be wrong with the majority than to be right alone.

   —John Kenneth Galbraith, American economist

T HE IDEA THAT MARKETS are the best aggregators of dispersed information runs counter to almost all our beliefs about group meetings, survey results, the role of experts, and the way organizations ought to work. Market-based business decisions are often more accurate than those provided by any other method. In part, these good results come from the virtues of markets; in part, they reflect the problems implicit in each of the other methods.

The most common of these other methods is, as Dave Barry notes, meetings. There are also polls and surveys, and reliance on experts. Mathematicians and statisticians offer predictions based on quantitative analysis. Each method has its own self-interested set of insiders, loyal to their preferred method.

Some of society's most important decisions are made by groups of people getting together to deliberate. Parliaments and juries try to find the right answer, or at least the best answer. Every business has marketing groups, planners, and boards of directors sitting through endless meetings. We assume these gatherings produce wise judgment and good decisions. And they seem democratic. If we asked the organizers of a meeting to explain why it is being held, they would probably think for a moment, and then reply that one or more group members might have the right answer for the problem on the agenda. They trust that information and experience is spread among members and that the group decision will be as good as that of its most knowledgeable member. Even when no one in the group has much experience relevant to the problem, whoever called the meeting will trust that somehow the group will brainstorm to something useful.

But there are problems with the dynamics of any meeting. The first relates to the group's lack of cognitive diversity. Most people work with, and go to meetings with, others who are similar in age, background, education, experience, and worldview. This homogeneity undermines the ability to make quality decisions; the group is unlikely to incorporate multiple perspectives and experiences. Brooke Harrington, a researcher at the Max Planck Institute, analyzed investment groups and concluded, "The larger the proportion of friendship and other socioeconomic ties within a group, the worse its portfolio performs."

There are usually lots of commonalities. A survey by Arnold Wood, president of Martingale Asset Management, and John Payne, a professor of psychology at Duke University, found that 85 percent of investment committee members were white males over fifty years old. There were no members under the age of thirty; only 15 percent were female, and only 5 percent were minorities.

The other common problem with the dynamics of a meeting is the information cascade. The first few individuals to state an opinion may provide information supporting only one side of an issue. Later speakers conform to the consensus of the cascade.

Cascades can also be hierarchical (or reputational). This happens when individuals go along with higher-ranking speakers to maintain their reputation as team players. Individuals caught in either an informational or hierarchical cascade don't speak up and reveal their own private information and so the final decision does not reflect the collective knowledge of the group.

Remember the Millennium Bug, and how the cascade of information about it predicted chaos? On January 1, 2000, computers were going to malfunction because pre-1980 software coded a year by the last two digits only. On the first day of the new millennium, the year 2000 would be read as 1900. Elevators would stop running because they had not been serviced for a hundred years. X-ray machines would go berserk, and aircraft would fall from the sky. So many passengers postponed travel that Western airlines cancelled two-thirds of the long-haul flights that would have been in the air at midnight on the final day of the twentieth century.

While most software engineers privately argued that the fears were baseless, they were silenced by the cascade and said nothing publicly. Small armies of novice programmers were hired and taught obsolete programming languages, Fortran and Cobol, so they could rewrite old software and fix the problem. The Millennium came, and sure enough, the software that had been fixed did not malfunction. Neither did the unfixed software. The Millennium Bug debacle taught us more about information cascades than about obsolete software.

Another example of informational and reputational cascades at work occurred during the 2002 pre-invasion debate on whether Iraq was developing weapons of mass destruction. Politicians and intelligence officials in every Western country were so convinced that WMD programs existed that all evidence to the contrary was suppressed or ignored. In Iraq, NATO WMD teams searched for months and found nothing. UK intelligence agencies later admitted possessing "no WMD" information, but the UK government had publicly adopted the US Central Intelligence Agency's pro-WMD position.

A prediction market reached the "no WMD" conclusion well before the US government. In early 2003, at the time of the coalition invasion of Iraq, TradeSports.com offered a set of contracts that paid off if WMD were found in Iraq by various dates. In March, the contract indicated a 70 percent chance of WMD. Over a six-month period, the probability dropped to zero. No one would invest in weapons being found, even at a 7 percent level. Trading in the contract was halted—at a time when US government news releases were still pointing to imminent WMD finds.

A cascade does not require an issue as serious as WMD, and can occur even with enlightened management. Several months prior to the January 2010 launch of Apple's iPad, the chosen product name was announced by Steve Jobs at an internal strategy meeting. Senior executives smiled and applauded. One account reported that the two women present at the meeting rolled their eyes and shook their heads, but said nothing. Weeks later, jokes about "Why use the Maxi Pad when the iPad is available?" hit the media. "#1 Tampon" became the #2 topic on Twitter.

What could the fourth or tenth speakers at the meeting do but agree with Steve Jobs? What female Apple employee would interrupt her distinguished chairman to risk being the only person in the room to suggest his new product certainly rhymes with iPod and iPhone, but also conjures an image of female hygiene use? She and everyone else in the meeting make a quick cost-benefit calculation on whether it makes sense to disagree with your CEO. Bucking the cascade means at best she will receive a small portion of the credit for a good solution. More likely, she will suffer reputational injury for disrupting the consensus.

The logical response is not to disclose. That is the cascade problem that a prediction market overcomes. The iPad logo took on its own meaning and eclipsed the joke once the product was released, but the initial connotation probably would have come as a surprise to Mr. Jobs and other men in the meeting.

A great example of why groups should predict in secret rather than vote in public comes from the same Michael Mauboussin, who runs Academy Award markets with his MBA students at Columbia University. Keep in mind that Mauboussin is one of the most respected people in the field of finance, and has written extensively on how to make good decisions. Here's the story:

A number of years ago, I was on a committee that was voting on whether to bring a person into the organization. After hearing the balance of the evidence on the candidate, I was in favor of bringing him in. The committee chair then started going around the conference table, asking for a verbal yea or nay on whether we approved of the candidate.

It so happened that the man sitting next to me was a physicist who had won the Nobel Prize and is probably the smartest person I have ever met. He was to vote right before me, and offered a nay when the chair called on him. So here I was, set to say yea, but faced with the world's smartest man saying nay only seconds before. Feeling seriously conflicted; I said nay and slumped in my chair.

Mauboussin adds, "By going around the room as he did, the chair invited social conformity and reduced independence."

A Web-based experiment by Columbia University psychologists Matthew Salganik, Peter Dodds, and Duncan Watts illustrates how biasing it can be to even think you know how others will decide. The researchers asked thousands of Web viewers to predict what songs on a list would be most successful. Some predictors were shown just the song title and the name of the band. Other predictors were also shown how often each song had been downloaded. When predictors knew what songs were most popular, those became more popular in their own judgment. They judged unpopular songs as—well, unpopular. Peer pressure ruled even when the predictors had no idea who their peers were.

Peer pressure and bullying are what causes the failure of many focus groups, which tend to be dominated by their loudest and most opinionated members. The long-running television comedy *Seinfeld* had four separate test episodes flop with four different focus groups. It was "too Jewish and too hip." The few who hated the show were more vocal and determined than the many who thought it to be pretty funny.

If meetings and other deliberations are imperfect, maybe a survey is a good way to provide information. Ask a question of a large group of people, and assume that the majority answers or the average answer is correct. All that needs to be decided is who has good information, how to reach them, and how to motivate them to think seriously about the issue rather than brushing off the surveyor with a snap response.

It turns out that each of those requirements causes problems. The biggest challenge is that it's often impossible, and certainly expensive, to identify and then reach out to everyone with appropriate knowledge. The only feasible option is to ask the question to a sample of people, and to project that answer to the entire population. This is how election polls are carried out.

Sampling part of the population and assuming that the answer represents the whole population is a good solution, if it works. The theory behind sampling was illustrated in 1685 by mathematician Jakob Bernoulli. He asked readers to imagine a large jar with black and white pebbles in a certain proportion to each other. He wanted to estimate the correct proportion of black to white pebbles, but without the easy expedient of dumping the jar.

Bernoulli's answer was to sample. He pulled out one black pebble. The next was white, then another white, then three blacks. As more pebbles were sampled, what Bernoulli called "the law of large numbers" takes effect, and the proportion of pebbles in the sample becomes a good estimate of the proportion in the jar. Depending on how many pebbles he pulled out, Bernoulli could estimate how close the sample would be to the actual ratio of black and white pebbles in the jar.

Bernoulli's sampling idea works as long as there are no biases as to which pebbles you draw—for example, the black pebbles are larger with rough surfaces, and the white are smaller and smooth. If there is bias, sampling is unreliable. When you sample humans rather than pebbles, there always is bias.

Sampling bias led to the *Chicago Daily Tribune*'s infamous headline following the 1948 presidential election, "Dewey Defeats Truman." It wasn't just the *Daily Tribune* that blew the call; virtually every newspaper and every public opinion poll predicted that incumbent president Harry S. Truman would be defeated by Republican Thomas E. Dewey, and by a landslide. By noon the day after voting, it was clear that Truman had won.

What happened? Most political surveys were, at the time, conducted by telephone. Pollsters failed to account for the fact that telephones were expensive and owned primarily by the more affluent fraction of the population, who also, disproportionately, supported the Republican Party and Mr. Dewey. The *Daily Tribune* had pulled a lot of large, rough black pebbles from the urn without noticing they were different from the smaller, smooth white ones.

A more recent example comes from presidential Election Day exit polling, still a favorite technique of television commentators. These surveys ask a sample of people leaving a polling place to reveal how they just voted. It sounds like an obvious and valid idea, but it turns out to also be prone to bias. In the 2004 US presidential election, early television network–run exit polls showed John Kerry beating George Bush by three points. On the basis of these results, two national networks jumped the gun and announced Kerry's likely victory. It turned out Democrats were more willing to reveal how they voted—or more willing to talk to a stranger asking personal questions—than were Republicans. Bush won handily.

One of the safest predictions I can offer is that a decade from now, polling as we know it, and in particular political polling, will have been substantially replaced by markets.

Perhaps we could bypass deliberation groups and surveys and rely on experts. This is the solution humans seem most comfortable with. We have a deep-rooted need to believe there are a few smart, or at least well-trained, people out there who can provide an answer. We hold experts in high esteem and defer to them. But we know from previous examples that experts are often outperformed by prediction markets. Why?

Experts like brain surgeons or chess masters certainly offer valuable answers, but in fairly narrow areas. Chess experts visualize future moves in a way that lesser players cannot. But their expertise does not extend beyond the game of chess. They would never be consulted for a problem in investing, or achieving high Scrabble scores. Even on areas where they are knowledgeable, experts may bring less information to a problem than the aggregate information available in a prediction group.

In broader areas of expertise—economics or politics or human psychology—we know that an expert (or a manager) trying to reach a decision suffers from the same cognitive distortions as do nonexperts. These include *confirmation bias*, which leads people to ignore evidence that contradicts existing knowledge; *anchoring,* which causes them to weigh one piece of information too heavily; and *risk aversion,* which renders them overly cautious. Daniel Kahneman points out in his 2011 book, *Thinking, Fast and Slow*, that one common bias among experts (and managers) is that when faced with a complex, difficult problem, they often choose to answer an easier one instead, without realizing it.

Perhaps more important, experts often simply don't know what they don't know. Experts have been shown to be consistently overconfident about their predictions, and often unwilling to change in the face of new evidence. Just like the rest of us.

Like crowds betting on horse races, experts overestimate the probability of unusual events and underestimate more common ones. For example, everyone—expert and novice—knows that storing a firearm in the home puts children at risk. Experts testify before congressional committees and municipal councils on the need for gun control, with the danger to children as the major concern. No one expresses as much concern about backyard swimming pools. However, economist Steven Levitt has calculated that if a household has both a gun and a swimming pool, a child in that household is about one hundred times more likely to die in the pool than by the gun.

A prediction market with investors who have both guns and a swimming pool might well flag this. Those who take part in such a market would bring the same biases about dangers to children as do experts. But the nature of the market is that biases average out. Market participants, knowing they are not expert, search for information. Those who have confidence in what they find invest more, and flag the dangers inherent in swimming pools.

If we are going to rely on experts, there is the problem of how to identify one. Remember my jellybean experiment (chapter 5)? When I ask my MBA class to identify the jellybean experts in their midst, or ask the experts to self-identify, no one can do it. For most prediction problems, a group knowledgeable enough to identify its experts probably does not need them.

Quantitative analysis is also used as a method of prediction, and is sometimes used as the basis for a prediction market. Quant analysis is math applied to issues that have occurred on multiple previous occasions. For some types of problems, quant analysis, either used alone or combined with a prediction market, yields better answers than almost any other technique.

There are many examples of problems that are best handled by quant analysis. Michael Lewis's best-selling book *Moneyball* describes the success of the low-budget Oakland As baseball team. Baseball is a sport with lots of what are called counting statistics: home runs, batting average, wins, and strikeouts. Lewis describes how instead of relying on scouting and statistics, Oakland used a quant formula that measured a player's offensive capability by the number of runs he created. Runs created are times on base (hits plus walks plus being hit by a pitched ball), multiplied by total bases, divided by times at-bat plus walks.

When offensive capability numbers from a past season are put in the equation, it accurately predicts the number of runs the team scored that year. The runs-created stat quantifies what a team tries to accomplish with its times at bat. The formula does things no scout does, giving credit to a player who has the patience to wait out a walk, or who is brave or stupid enough to stand in and get hit by a pitch.

This quant approach was introduced by Harvard graduate Paul De-Podesta, who was hired by general manager Billy Beane to exploit the lack of good decision making by baseball experts. Scouts accessed future player success by whether cognitive examples of that type of player were readily available to them: "swings like Brooks Robinson," or "fields like Roberto Alomar." Good prospect results that did not readily match an existing cognitive example were explained with imaginary concepts: "momentum," "seeing the ball well," or "the intangibles."

The approach was DePodesta's answer to baseball's consistent mispricing of players. It offered a breakthrough in a problem every major league team agonizes over. How do you predict, prior to the annual player draft, which prospects are most likely to be successful at the major league level? Throughout most of baseball history, the answer was to have retired major league players attend lots of high school and college games each year to watch players perform.

Does this approach work? Despite the experience and expertise of these scouts, only one player in six drafted in the first ten rounds of the draft makes it to the majors for as much as one full season. Oakland's quant approach allowed the team to draft a higher proportion of future major leaguers than would a reliance on scouts—and more important, a higher proportion than its wealthier competitors the New York Yankees, Boston Red Sox, and Los Angeles Dodgers. Until the rest of the league caught on and caught up, DePodesta and Beane used their drafting insight to make the playoffs four years in a row, from 2000 to 2003.

Quant can be sexy. Brad Pitt played Billy Beane in the movie version of *Moneyball*, released in the fall of 2011.

A more recent quant approach to baseball comes from Bloomberg, a New York company that produces sophisticated financial software. On the urging of analyst Bo Moon and manager Stephen Orban, the company launched player-evaluation software in December 2009. This might seem pretty far from its core Wall Street business, but as explained by Bloomberg president Daniel Doctoroff, "If you think of players as securities and teams as portfolios then our infrastructure for managing information about securities and portfolios could be adapted to sports."

Teams use the Bloomberg software to evaluate free agents—players no longer under contract to their former professional team. The software assigns values to positions played, pitches per plate appearance, home runs, on-base percentage, and eleven other areas of performance. Tell the software what you want in a free agent—defense, power hitting, and leadership—and it ranks the top ten available players for each position you are looking to strengthen. Divide the ranking by the cost of the player and you have a shopping list for free agents ranked by what you need and can afford.

Another well-known quant example involves chess grand master and former world champion Garry Kasparov, who was defeated in a widely publicized May 1997 game against an IBM computer nicknamed Deep Blue. What the computer had going for it was a memory containing 700,000 grand master games. The program evaluated any board position in terms of what grand masters who subsequently won had played from that position. Kasparov's experience lost to a quant program and a large database.

Could a market composed of humans be used to choose the best moves in a game of chess against a grand master? Actually this has been done, and with great success. In 1999, Kasparov played an Internet game "against the world." Four chess experts suggested possible moves from each position during the game. World players came from fifteen countries. Each member of the market, the moderately skilled and the rank beginner alike, followed the game online and was allowed one vote on each move. The majority prediction on each move became the World Team's choice. Some participants dropped out and became observers as board positions evolved beyond their ability to analyze.

The World Team had two days to predict each new "best move." The game took four months to play and was in doubt until the fiftieth move. Kasparov prevailed in the end game, and called this "the greatest game in the history of chess." The aggregated predictions of a number of players who had never met, none of whom likely to be anywhere near Kasparov's skill or experience level, were almost equal to the expertise of the master. In the opinion of many chess observers, the World Team played a more creative game than did Deep Blue.

Other successes come from combining a quant model and a prediction market. An example you will find familiar flashes on my computer monitor when I log on to Amazon.com. My greeting screen says, "Hello Don Thompson . . . We've noticed that customers who have purchased *I Bought Andy Warhol* by Richard Polsky also purchased *Late Mamluk*

Patronage by Khaled A. Alhamzah." This is a book on the art and architecture of one period of Middle Eastern history, and would seem to have little to do with Warhol's *Red Marilyn.*

Amazon uses a *collaborative filter;* it recommends books purchased by customers who have bought at least two books that I have. Other sites do similar filtering. MSNBC.com remembers the articles that I have read online and recommends new articles accessed by others with the same interests.

Amazon applies a quant model to the output of an unconscious prediction market, where others cast a ballot without realizing they are voting. They vote by reading what I read, then investing in a new book. A compilation of these purchases generates a prediction of what I might want to purchase. Yes, I ordered the Alhamzah book.

A more elaborate collaborative filter and unconscious prediction market is used by retailer figleaves.com. A shopper logs on to the figleaves.com site on a Saturday morning to look for a pair of women's silk slippers. Eight seconds later, and unbidden, a pop-up window shows her a man's bathrobe. About 30 percent of the time, the shopper is also looking for a present for a man. She is surprised, and may even be pleased.

The technology, from ATG (for Art Technology Group), a Cambridge, Massachusetts, data-crunching firm, tracks online visitors. It knows that 30 percent of women shopping on a Saturday morning, and of an age and demographic that looks for silk slippers, are likely to be shopping for a man as well as for themselves. Figleaves knows that the same woman shopping on a Tuesday morning is probably in a hurry. She may log on from the office, and is unlikely to be looking for a present for a man. On Tuesday she won't be shown any pop-up ads. Nor will she be shown pop-ups on a Saturday morning if she first clicks on Figleaves' cosmetics section. Previous clicks by shoppers tell ATG that cosmetic shoppers are not looking for gifts.

The 70 percent of Saturday morning shoppers who look at silk slippers but are not interested in a man's gift must also be considered. The previous Web clicks of those nonbuyers tells Figleaves that if it shows the robe in one corner of the screen rather than full-screen, and makes it easy to cancel the pop-up, only about 5 percent of shoppers will be annoyed enough to immediately log off.

Quant models come into play in situations when there is simply too much information for other techniques to handle. This is the opposite of garbage-in, garbage-out. There is a tsunami of information in, confusion out. Stephen Baker's 2008 book, *The Numerati*, provides an example. Baker tells the story of Syrian-born mathematician Samer Takriti, who headed up an IBM team of forty PhDs developing a mathematical model of the company's fifty thousand tech consultants. The goal was to inventory the skills, experience, and idiosyncrasies of each employee so that the computer could assist in predicting how they should be assigned to clients across industries and countries.

The quant model looked at each person's corporate successes: projects brought in on time and on budget, plus the characteristics of each other collaborator on the successful projects. Online calendars provided input on how workers used their time; cell phone call records and e-mail copy lists showed relationships and social networks. The model looked at languages spoken, level of religious belief, dietary restrictions, concerns about air pollution (scratch Beijing and Cairo), spousal flexibility (eliminate Tehran), and perhaps, enemies within the company (reinstate Tehran).

A more traditional prediction market, where investors knew each employee personally, would have done a good job of assigning twenty-five people to projects. Could it have assigned fifty thousand? Not very likely; it would have been tsunami-in, confusion-out.

Where prediction markets have been used to supplement meetings or other forms of prediction, they have found great success. My all-time favorite corporate prediction market, Rite-Solutions, is discussed in chapter 1. Case histories of innovative and successful use of markets by Google, Best Buy, Misys, Hewlett-Packard, and other organizations follow.

PART TWO

What Can Business Markets Do?

7

Google

*Creativity is no longer about which companies have the
most visionary executives, but who has the most compelling
"architecture of participation"; which companies make it easy,
interesting, and rewarding for a wide range of contributors to offer
ideas, solve problems, and improve products.*

—Tim O'Reilly, CEO, O'Reilly Media, referring to Google

THERE IS A GREAT corporate prediction market success story where the ideal blend of organization culture plus active support from top management came together—this company embedded a prediction market as part of its DNA. Every time you access Google, you enter a complex prediction market. The company name is derived from *googol*, meaning 10 to the power of 100. That is a one, followed by a hundred zeros. It is intended to represent a very large search process.

In 1998, company founders Sergey Brin and Larry Page took a leave of absence from Stanford University's doctoral program to build a commercial search engine. They wanted to name it *Googol*, but registered *Google* at the trademark office. When later told they had misspelled the term, they again tried to register *Googol*, but discovered it was taken—so they stuck with the mistake (the alternative was to revert to the company's original name, *BackRub*, coined for the search engine's ability to analyze "back links" that point to a particular website). The verb *google* was added to the Oxford English Dictionary in 2006.

What does Google do? The company's chief economist Hal Varian describes it as a "yenta." Every fan of the musical *Fiddler on the Roof* knows that *yenta* is a Yiddish term for matchmaker. In *Fiddler*, Yenta matched two young women, Chava and Hodel, with men who were (hopefully) scholars, handsome, and rich. On the Internet, Google matches people searching for information with providers; it also matches those offering a product or service with those looking to buy.

Google started in 1998, when the dominant search engines were Yahoo!, Lycos, and Alta Vista. These produced really ugly results, with lots of meaningless information. Each worked by looking at the text of a document and counting how many times it contained a word or phrase. If you searched for "Stanford University," the search engine produced a list of documents containing that word, including a long list of merchants on the northern California city's University Avenue. Website operators found it easy to game these search engines. A vendor of sex videos would include the term "Stanford University" (and hundreds of similar terms) at the bottom of each Web page, guaranteeing a prominent position in front of the eyes of seekers of higher education.

Within a year of its 1998 launch, Google had become the default search engine for most users. In 2010, it performed 9 billion searches a month. For each search, it scans 32 billion pages—a stack of paper seventy-five miles high—in about two-fifths of a second. Until mid-2009, when Microsoft introduced its *Bing* search engine, Google was unquestionably best at putting the right information at the top of the search page.

What does this have to do with a prediction market? Google does the best job of predicting which documents are most valuable for a particular search term because it uses what past searchers for that term have predicted as being best. Searchers invest time and contribute expertise to produce more accurate results for the next user, without realizing they are involved in a prediction market. Some individuals conduct smart searches, others are less smart. As with Galton's ox or horse race betting, the smart and the naive together produce a good prediction.

The conceptual breakthrough came from Larry Page. This was the idea that not all Internet sites are created equal; a link from a search term to a major news site matters more than a link to an obscure blog. Google weighs each link by the score of the site connecting to it.

Google looks at how many people have linked to a Web page, and what text they used to make the link. Whichever page has the highest number of weighted votes for the topic being searched goes to the top of the list the next time that term is searched. The second-highest vote total places second. Each time a viewer accesses a page and then goes to a second, Google records this as a vote that the second page is relevant to the content of the first page. Pages that have many previous hits are awarded more votes than those that have few. Larry Page called the software *PageRank.*

Google superimposes a personal search feature on PageRank that uses your past search queries and clicks to predict what it should offer on your next search. If Bill Gates and Martha Stewart were each to enter the search term "blackberry," Gates would, it is said, get pages related to the Black-Berry mobile device, while Stewart would get references to fruit. But what the interest-prediction software delivers is even more subtle than this example suggests. About nine times in ten, the software can determine whether someone who enters the search term "apple" is talking about that company's products or about the fruit.

Google also lets users vote on the order in which ads appear on the right side of each Google screen. Instead of ranking ads according to how much each advertiser offers, Google ranks them on a combination of how much the vendor pays and how frequently users click on the ad. The ad at the top may pay less per click than others lower down, but makes up for it with more clicks. Each click is a user's prediction that this ad is relevant to those who entered the search term.

A good ad click-through rate is about 3 percent. Of those who click through to read the advertiser's material, about 3 percent buy something. One person in a thousand who sees the ad will buy the product. That sounds pathetic, but search engine ads are actually such an effective form of promotion that advertisers pay well for placement. In 2010, Google's total revenue was $29.3 billion, $10.4 billion of it pretax profit.

Google followed PageRank and ad positions by establishing an in-company prediction market. Eric Schmidt, then the chief executive of the company, and Bo Cowgill, then a Google strategist, had read James Surowiecki's *The Wisdom of Crowds.* In an internal posting promoting the market, Cowgill wrote, "By aggregating the number and nature of incoming links to a web page, Google already uses the collective genius of crowds to rank search results. Democracy on the web is part of our corporate culture. But PageRank isn't the only way to harness the collective intelligence of large groups. So I propose creating Google Decision Markets."

Every prediction market needs both innovators and an early champion. The Google innovators were Cowgill and four others he recruited: Ilya Kirnos, Doug Banks, Patri Friedman, and Piaw Na. These five Googlers (as employees refer to themselves) launched the Google Prediction Market (GPM) and built the information system to support it.

The champion was Hal Varian. Varian is a professor in the Haas School of Business at the University of California. Since 2003, he has been on leave at Google. Varian is probably the most respected information economics academic in the United States. *Fortune* magazine lists him at number nine on their list of the top fifty business intellectuals, and lists his book *Information Rules* as one of the seventy-five best strategy books ever.

Varian's opinion carries a lot of weight with Sergey Brin and Larry Page. Varian sat in on GPM-planning meetings and contributed the essential stamp of approval. The GPM took off in April 2005. The mandate was to forecast product launch dates, new office openings, and almost anything of strategic importance to the company.

Google turned out to be a perfect organization to launch a prediction market. Unlike most companies, where managers think of ways to make money and then create products, Google has a culture where inventors think first of how to solve problems and then come up with ways to make money from the solutions. Any new way to identify and solve problems fits well with the Google culture. Google tolerates wildly out-of-the-box thinking and experimentation on nonsearch products; think of Gmail and Google Maps. Marissa Mayer, Google's twentieth employee, first female engineer, and now vice president of Location and Local Services, says 80 percent of new Google products will fail; the other 20 percent will be memorable. There is no focus on sure bets.

Google budgets for innovation with the way it allocates employee time. Technical employees spend 80 percent of their time on core search and advertising businesses, the other 20 percent on projects of their own choosing. Managers spend 70 percent on the core business, 10 percent on entirely new businesses and products, and 20 percent on related but different projects. During one six-month period, fifty new products—half the new Google product launches during that period—evolved from this 20 percent time. These included Gmail, AdSense, and Google News. One Googler used his 20 percent time to add a Google search interface in the Klingon language. Cowgill and his four colleagues built GPM during their 20 percent time.

About a third of Google's prediction markets involve the company: "Will Google open a Moscow office?" "Will the beta version of this new product debut on time?" "Will Google Talk's quality score increase?" One-third involve demand forecasting: "How many new users will sign up for Gmail in the next three months?"

Of the other third, half involve things that could have an impact on Google: "Will Apple release an Intel-based Mac?" "Will the Firefox Web browser's market share increase by 10 percent?" The only questions that are absolutely off-limits are those dealing with the company stock price or with quarterly earnings. These might turn Googler investors into insiders for security law purposes.

The remaining questions are for fun and motivation: "Which team will win the NBA finals?" "Who will become the Apprentice?" "Will *Star Wars* episode III rock?" When employees gain experience in fun markets, they move to questions of project completion and demand forecasting.

Google found that prices in these markets are accurate predictors (see figure 7-1). It plotted prices against the likelihood of a prediction coming true in the same way Inkling did. At the time it did the chart, GPM had run 280 prediction markets, with 1,500 investors and 80,000 trades.

WHAT CAN BUSINESS MARKETS DO?

FIGURE 7-1

Accuracy of the Google prediction market

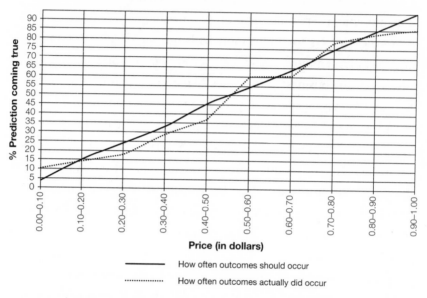

Price (in dollars)

—————— How often outcomes should occur

················· How often outcomes actually did occur

Source: Bo Cowgill, *Google as a Prediction Market*, a presentation at the O'Reilly Money Tech Conference, New York, February 2008, http://googleblog.blogspot.com/2005/09/putting-crowd-wisdom-to-work.html.

The horizontal axis in figure 7-1 indicates the last trading price; the vertical axis is how often the predicted result happened. The straight line represents how often outcomes should actually occur. Predict a probability of 0.8, and the event should happen 80 percent of the time. The jagged line is how often they did happen. As with the Intrade graph, the two lines are remarkably close. Google predictions are considered correct about 90 percent of the time.

Equally important, GPMs spot the likely outcome very early. As much as ten weeks before the closing date of the market, the highest-stock-price outcome is the one most likely to occur. GPM predictions are also decisive; the stock price of the most likely outcome increases and all other outcomes decrease as more information comes to the market.

The aggregated predictions from Google employees are often better than those from the company's in-house experts. Where trading volumes are high—for questions like whether Microsoft would purchase Yahoo!—predictive accuracy is greater. And investors learn over time. The longer employees invest in the GPM, the more likely they are to have a successful trading record. An interesting caveat to this is that an employee's performance in the GPM declines above a certain level in the corporate hierarchy. Perhaps the higher you rise, the more your thinking parallels existing company doctrine and the less you invest out of the box?

Hal Varian says of the market, "I expected this to be accurate because there is a lot of literature and experience with these systems. But this has been even better than I expected." The Google results and the resulting publicity energized a hundred other organizations to investigate prediction markets.

Google allows staff members at all levels to trade in these markets, and to trade on inside information. The company avoids possible violation of federal gambling laws by using virtual money called Goobles (Google rubles). Each investor receives ten thousand Goobles every three months, issued in weekly installments to avoid the possibility that investors who receive all their Goobles up front might invest immediately, lock in their positions, and do little future trading.

Goobles are redeemed for tickets on an in-house lottery, one ticket for each Gooble held at the end of a quarter. Six tickets are drawn at random, each paying $1,000. The most active trader each quarter gets $1,000. Other traders get gift certificates and special T-shirts. Total prize cost per quarter is $10,000, an average of $40 per trader.

Use of the lottery eliminates a problem that might arise from resetting the market at the end of a period. Without the lottery, an ambitious trader might *longshot*—invest by purchasing a low-probability outcome with whatever Goobles he had left at the end of the quarter ("Toronto Raptors to win the NBA championship") in the hope of earning huge returns.

If the Raptors did not win, the trader would lose all his Goobles but suffer no actual financial loss. He would begin the next quarter with a new allotment of ten thousand Goobles. The lottery encourages people to trade intelligently and end the quarter with as many Goobles as possible. It reflects the key consideration in market design: the rules must motivate investors to trade based on their real beliefs about outcomes of events represented by market securities.

What are the long-term implications for investors who take part? If a Googler loses Goobles—and everyone sees that she is losing—does that imply that she lacks management potential? Are the investors who make money the ones with promise? Google employees seem to think they are, but many who lose money still invest next period.

The five founding Googlers debated whether to allow insiders to trade. For many questions asked in a corporate prediction market, there are employees within the firm who have worked on the problem and possess inside information. Should Googlers working on Gmail be allowed to invest in a market asking: "How many Gmail users will there be at the end of the quarter?" The obvious reaction is that, like public stock markets, a prediction market must be free of insider trading.

That obvious answer is wrong. The goal of the GPM is not to level the playing field, but to produce the best possible predictions. To do this, you need to encourage those investors with the most accurate information to trade. If insiders simply repeat their department forecasts, they provide incentive for others to earn Goobles by bringing security prices back to where they should be. Google wants individual investors to invest against the project they are working on, if they think "against" is the right answer.

Since its inception, the GPM has had the problem that only a small proportion of employees take part. During the third quarter of 2010, 7,100 employees had a prediction market account, a low number considering there were at that time 23,000 sophisticated and technically adept Googlers. Only 1,625 placed a trade on one of the thirty contracts offered during the period. Markets work better with more participants; larger numbers make it easier to execute a trade without causing much movement in the price. So how do you get more Googlers to register and trade?

Cowgill's approach was not to offer more money, but to make trading more social and more open. He and his colleagues spent a lot of time thinking about incentives. Patri Friedman argued that a chance at $1,000 is not that meaningful to employees with six-figure salaries. Rather, he said, "Google is a T-shirt economy; people will volunteer for all sorts of things, and do work for other teams just to get a cool T-shirt."

There is evidence to support the value of this reputation-based reward system. In 2006 the outcome of the World Cup Football tournament was included in the GPM—but timing of the final caused announcement of winners to be delayed two weeks. When he sent out the list of winners, Cowgill forgot to announce who had won the cash prizes. Not a single Googler noticed. But e-mails flowed in asking when the shirts would be delivered.

A few weeks later, Cowgill received an investor complaint: "You said my rank was higher than number 20 but I did not get a shirt." It turned out the writer was removed from the shirt list because he also won $1,000. The concern about T-shirts was the reason Cowgill realized he had never identified those who won cash.

Cowgill did not get around to announcing the cash prizes for another month. Still no one asked. GPM investors only wanted to know about reputational prizes: their ranking in the system and the T-shirt that identified their status.

The GPM so far remains internal, except for a few questions contractors and vendors are invited to take part in. The limitation on investors provides further protection against the remote chance of the company being charged with running a gambling establishment. But Google must wonder if caution is worth the cost. Think of the innovative ideas that would come from opening the GPM to other Silicon Valley geeks!

Google discovered that the GPM produced the unintended benefit of expanding employees' personal connections. Employees from different departments were more likely to meet others who also took part in GPM. The market is a "conversation among employees," Cowgill says. "The conversation happens without politics and no one has an incentive to kiss up, fudge the numbers, or sandbag. Participants don't know who is on the other side of their position—a coworker, the masseuse, or Sergey Brin."

Bo Cowgill and economists Eric Zitzewitz and Justin Wolfers have worked with Google data to determine what systematic biases might exist in GPM results. One is a bias toward optimism. Predictions of high sales ranges for Google products are overpriced by 10 percent. Optimism is more prevalent with newly hired employees and more evident on days when Google stock is appreciating. This is not surprising. New Googlers come to the campus full of enthusiasm; at an early point in their Google career they receive stock options. Google employees with longer tenure and more trading experience show less optimistic bias—so markets should perform better as collective experience increases.

At the 2008 meetings of the American Economic Association, Bo Cowgill presented the results of a study on how Googlers share information. Google knows the GPS location of every desk in every one of its offices. It knows if that desk is in a cubicle or an open area. It knows when employees move to a new desk location. Using this data, Cowgill determined that investors in the same physical location tend to make the same trades at the same time. Investment decisions by cube-mates are the best predictor of future trading decisions by others in the cube. A Googler who changes location and changes cube-mates changes behavior as well.

Beliefs at Google are clustered not by social or language or ethnic groupings or by what university degree Googlers hold, but by physical proximity measured in distance between desks. There is some relationship among professional and social contacts, but these are much less important than the effect of physical proximity. This finding reinforces Eric Schmidt and Hal Varian's famous third rule for managing knowledge workers: "Pack Them In."

They are packed in. Sergey Brin and Larry Page share an office. Former CEO Eric Schmidt shared one with a software engineer. Hal Varian and Bo Cowgill shared a cubicle until Cowgill left Google in 2009 to enter the business PhD program at Berkeley.

Beyond the GPM, the whole Google search engine is a prediction market exercise, where everyone in a "tribe" votes on that tribe's preferences. This unconscious voting takes place when Google processes the information you seek or the sites you visit online.

Each time you visit the website of a restaurant or bar, you vote for that establishment. If you spend longer on the site, your vote is more important. Because Google usually knows where you come from, it can map behavior by what sites the tribe of people like you look for or spend time at. What are the popular New York restaurants for business travelers from Evanston, a prosperous suburb of Chicago? What bars does this tribe go to while visiting Manhattan? Should a Google ad for that New York bar be provided to all members of the Evanston tribe who google the name of any Manhattan restaurant?

Sense Networks, a New York analytics firm, has picked up on this prediction idea and expanded tribal mapping using mobile phone information. The company's Citysense software tracks where you live, shop, and eat. When you move around with your mobile phone turned on, you are in touch with cell towers or Wi-Fi networks that feed your location to a global positioning system.

This is the system that tells the phone company where you are when you originate a call, so it can bill you correctly. The same system allows the GPS in your car to pinpoint your location in an unfamiliar part of the city. Google's Latitude application uses this information to allow phone subscribers with the required Google download to locate partners and friends. Are they stuck in traffic? Are they still at work? What are they doing over on the east side of town?

Citysense uses the GPS capability to track people with mobile phones as they move across the city. If you sleep on Smith Street in Long Island City most nights, you probably live there, and Citysense can determine your postal code. From aggregated census and other data, this gives the company a good take on your religion, household income, marital status, number of children, educational level, and the size of your backyard garden. (That is why so many online sites just ask for your postal code in order to enter.) If you fall into a "middle age with higher income and Jewish" demographic, you won't be annoyed by flashing Web ads for poker sites—because you are unlikely to ever gamble.

When you visit Manhattan, the firm's analysts know the restaurants, bars, and hotels you vote for, based on where you choose to go. Are you loyal to one restaurant and bar each day of your visit, or do you make a new choice each day? Do members of your Long Island City tribe prefer MoMA, the Metropolitan Museum, or the Guggenheim?

How would you use an involuntary market to predict what evening of the week offers the best chance to meet a new, loving partner? OkCupid, a matchmaking service, recently tried to answer that question. First, it categorized a "sexually available" subset of its members, based on answers to four questions that seemed to point to openness to new relationships. The questions asked about sex as a "romantic priority," "expressed willingness to sleep with someone on a first date," and self-identifying as "extraverted" and "adventurous." The movements of this "available" group were then tracked through cell phones in New York City, Washington, DC, and Boston. So what day offers the most options for singles on the prowl? Wednesday. Thursday is second, then Saturday, then Friday. Would a survey have identified that?

If your mobile phone exchanges signals with a tower, your location can be pinpointed within about 200 yards (180 meters). Most current handsets, including BlackBerry, iPhone, and Nokia, use the 120 million Wi-Fi net nodes now in place around the world. These can locate you to within 25 feet (7 meters). The GPS limit is expected to be 3 feet (1 meter) by late 2012.

If you have a Citysense application on your New York City mobile phone, you can press a "Locate me" icon to see the top five places people like you go from where you are now. Google is researching how to combine its technology with this type of cell phone information as another way of helping predict the advertising they should feature when you enter a certain term in the search engine.

Google made one costly decision before GPM was put in place. The company announced in early 2004—a year before the GPM—that it would do an initial public offering (IPO) of its stock in August of that year. The Iowa Electronic Markets launched a prediction market to estimate the "right" share offering price and to see if a market could predict this as accurately as the Morgan Stanley and Credit Suisse First Boston investment bankers who were advising Google.

IPO pricing is both important and difficult. In spite of the millions of dollars in fees that investment bankers receive, there is systematic underpricing of these new issues. Underpricing means that the issue price is lower than the first-day trading price when the security is listed on an exchange. Money is left on the table; the issuing company could have charged more. Think of the infamous eBay and Amazon.com IPOs.

To minimize the risk of mispricing, Google conducted a form of Dutch auction before the stock was priced. Potential investors were required to tell an investment dealer how many shares they would buy and the price they were willing to pay. Google provided an estimated price range, but the investor could bid lower or higher. The two investment banks used the price offers to allocate shares and set the IPO price.

Even with the Dutch auction process, investment bankers recommended a too-low price. Google's August 2004 IPO raised $1.4 billion, with fees of $45 million for the investment bankers. The final Iowa Electronic Markets share price prediction was 4 percent above the closing price on the first day of trading. Had Google priced at the IEM price rather than that suggested by its investment bankers, it would have sold 10 percent fewer shares but taken in an additional $200 million.

8

Best Buy

Ideas have an authenticity when they originate from the field.

—Bradley Anderson, former CEO, Best Buy

People make up this company; we believe in them, we are not afraid to listen to them.

—Bethany Kinsela, Best Buy executive

WITH 2010 SALES of $49 billion and operating profit of $1.1 billion, Best Buy is the largest retailer of consumer electronics in the world. Management quality at Best Buy is such that it has been named "Company of the Year" by *Forbes* magazine, and has made *Fortune* magazine's list of "Most Admired Companies." That does not suggest an organization where you would expect sales-floor employees to provide much input to top management. However, when it comes to corporate use of prediction markets, Best Buy is better known than Google. Best Buy's market wisdom is credited with insights that helped the company to prosper, while Circuit City crashed.

Best Buy employs 150,000 people, 115,000 of those in the United States, the others in Canada, Mexico, China, the United Kingdom, and continental Europe. Most are involved with customer contact on the sales floor. As is true of most retail enterprises, the company has a high employee turnover rate: 145 percent a few years ago, but down to 50 percent in 2011. Running a prediction market in this environment would seem far more difficult than at a company like Rite-Solutions or Google, with their stable, highly educated workforces.

In 2005, Jeff Severts, then a thirty-seven-year-old vice president of Consumer and Brand Marketing at Best Buy, proved it could be done. He started the prediction market that would later become known as Tag-Trade. He says he was motivated by the insight that "Big companies are like communist countries—we all know how well communist countries worked. At some point they fell apart, not because the leaders were dumb, but because nobody would tell the leaders at the top, who made decisions, what decisions to make."

Severts's initial motivation was to improve the forecasting system he inherited with his new VP position. Best Buy did its sales forecasting on a monthly rolling basis. Each of the eight buying teams contributed a forecast, and the eight forecasts were aggregated. The problem was that estimates were driven as much by human factors as by expected demand. The forecast figures were not just the basis for ordering merchandise, but also determined budgets, bonuses, and promotions. Executives wanted sales targets they could meet or beat. Setting targets too low meant that a manager might be criticized for overordering inventory. Underordering would bring criticism because there was unmet demand. A better system was needed, but there was resistance to change; executives thought they knew how to work within the existing system.

Like Eric Schmidt and Bo Cowgill at Google (see chapter 7), Severts was motivated by the ideas of James Surowiecki, who gave a management seminar at Best Buy and offered his familiar argument: "For predicting events driven by a large number of variables, a diverse group of company employees may produce better results than experts." Surowiecki used the example of a Best Buy department manager who noticed that customers were showing less enthusiasm for a particular brand of cell phone. A warehouse clerk might have spotted that trend even earlier through slower inventory turnover.

But neither manager nor clerk might have any incentive to pass that information up the corporate ladder. Surowiecki explained that a decision reached by a prediction market would not be subject to the same human distortions as Best Buy's current sales forecast system. Because employees have collective access to information, they could trigger an early heads-up to company buyers.

The insight Severts took away from Surowiecki's presentation went beyond creating a market to predict cell phone sales or reforming the sales forecast system he had inherited. Severts wanted his first prediction market to generate employee feedback on a more important Best Buy initiative: the company was in the process of reconfiguring each of its stores to target one of several types of customer.

Called *customer centricity*, this was a micro-market segmentation scheme that assigned each store to one or more categories: home theater geeks, soccer moms, average-Joe electronics shoppers, or middle America. At one extreme, Best Buy Store 952, in Baytown, Texas (just outside Houston), chose to focus on sales of electronics to Eastern European sailors on shore leave from cargo ships and oil tankers. Each store was asked to woo its groups with a customized product and service mix. For Store 952, this involved moving iPods and Apple laptops to the front of the store and pairing them with overseas power converters and simplified signage. Senior management promoted customer centricity to financial analysts as a way for the company to improve margins and build customer loyalty.

The customer centricity initiative required a major capital investment. Would there be adequate return on this investment? Given senior management's vocal support for the concept, doubters were unlikely to speak up. Customer centricity seemed like a great issue for the first Best Buy prediction market.

It wasn't. When Severts discussed the idea of using a market mechanism to question the chairman's position, he discovered the idea was so potentially career-limiting that no one wanted to be associated with it. Senior manager Mike Linton offered great advice: if you are going to test an idea, test it on yourself first. This was lesson number one in Severts's list of how to start a prediction market while minimizing hostility.

One of Severts's responsibilities was Best Buy's gift-card business, a fast-growing part of his portfolio. Forecasts of gift card sales did not get aggregated with other forecasts and sent up the hierarchy; they went only to him. Gift cards were the perfect "test it on yourself" market.

The initial step was a simple online survey. Severts sent an e-mail to 210 employees asking them to estimate how many gift cards Best Buy would sell in February 2005. The winner received a $50 gift card. Employees were given figures for actual gift card sales over the previous twelve months. Severts received 190 responses.

On March 4, February gift-card sales figures were available. Compared with actual sales, the conventional Best Buy forecast process was off by 5 percent. The average guess from the 190 market participants was off by one-half of 1 percent. Severts sent out an e-mail reporting the results, with the caption *The Crowd Wins*. The first response came from the company's director of forecasting. It was not congratulatory; she said her team had been humiliated. The gift-card market provided lesson number two: never allow market results to be interpreted as reflecting negatively on existing managers.

Severts quickly announced what he thought had happened. The official forecasting team was obviously more knowledgeable than the individual predictors who had taken part in the market. But the 190 market participants represented a much broader base of information and insight. He promised to run additional market-versus-experts tests, to check whether the gift-card experiment had been an anomaly.

But, Severts added, the result showed that "even a rudimentary survey strips away the filters that typically distort information as it moves higher in an organization." He was convinced that Best Buy's employees had information and insight that mirrored what he had learned from Surowiecki's talk.

Severts's second market test also took place online. He asked his volunteers to predict Best Buy's 2005 Black Friday-to-Christmas Eve sales. Black Friday is the day after Thanksgiving, and is supposed to represent the time when a retailer moves from yearly losses (in the red) to a yearly profit position (in the black). Severts gave his volunteers the 2004 sales figures for the same period and the year-over-year sales growth percentage for the first three months of 2005.

The holiday sales prediction exercise is an incredibly important task. A forecast that is too low results in lost profits because goods can't be re-ordered and restocked in time. A forecast that is too high leads to excess inventory—and consumer electronics quickly depreciate in value.

This was Severts's first chance to see whether a Best Buy market could forecast sales. His volunteers' predictions were not being compared to those of the forecast team, but to forecasts made by experts—the eight buying teams. This time, he allowed predictors to change their forecast each week over the fourteen-week period, to respond to new information and events. Those events turned out to include Hurricane Katrina and a major increase in oil prices.

For this prediction exercise, Severts doubled his prize offer to a $100 gift card. Three hundred and fifty volunteers took part at the start of the market. On January 6, 2006, the results were announced. Four months before Christmas, the forecasting experts had been 93 percent accurate and the prediction market 99.9 percent accurate. The experts' results improved slightly over time, reaching 94 percent on November 24, the day the market closed. The prediction market results got slightly worse over the same period, as the number of participants shrank to sixty, most of these from the head office marketing and finance groups. Even with smaller numbers, the prediction market was 98 percent accurate on November 24.

With results from the two tests, Severts had enough evidence to promote his market concept in company meetings. His much-cited presentation compared Best Buy to centrally planned economies in the Soviet Union and China and included images of Joseph Stalin and Mao Zedong. He described these leaders as being like those in large corporations. They were removed from the grass roots of their own organizations, and their subordinates were reluctant to tell them the truth. He offered markets as a methodology that would avoid the imperfect knowledge and biases that seemed to characterize conventional Best Buy forecasting. The prediction market proposal was accepted.

There was still the issue of which questions to ask. Best Buy, like most organizations, was assumed to have a strong taboo against any question that implied an important company initiative might not succeed. Offering or even taking part in a market where an investor could vote for failure might be viewed as betrayal. "Air cover" from top management was essential. This was lesson number three. Without that support, Severts said, "You'll find yourself trading on what kind of casserole we're having in the cafeteria on Thursday."

A related concern among Best Buy investors was that their managers might discover the identity of those who predicted a negative outcome. This concern diminished over time because participants were allowed to trade using pseudonyms, and it became accepted that only one person knew the true identity of traders.

In early 2006, Severts had the two market successes under his belt, and CEO Brad Anderson gave him $50,000 in prediction market seed money, with a free hand to experiment. Anderson was not convinced that a market would work, but he thought the experiment would reinforce a company culture of driving information from lower to higher levels of the pyramid.

Severts, along with ten volunteers, designed a stock-trading exercise to flag potential issues with company strategy. The market was promoted as a game using play-money prizes. Severts christened it TagTrade, after the large yellow price tag that is the company's symbol. Commercial provider Consensus Point supplied the software and offered consulting on how to manage the market mechanism.

In 2007, Severts was promoted to a new role as vice president for Services, managing the twenty thousand technicians known as the Geek Squad. A few months later Brian Jaedike became manager of company prediction markets.

Jaedike came to Best Buy with a finance degree. He worked in the finance department and had had early success in Best Buy's pilot markets, in part because he was one of the few participants who both understood and was comfortable with short-selling.

Jaedike also chose to move slowly. He developed a two-stage road map that led to TagTrade in its current form. Wave One was rolled out in December 2007 and involved headquarters employees and word-of-mouth promotion. Securities were traded on the US presidential race, housing prices, and sports, but nothing specific to the company. The conclusion from Wave One was that "populist assets"—those based on events attracting media attention—both sustained TagTrade trading and produced accurate results. That was lesson four.

For election, housing, and sports securities, the Wave One market results were accurate for eight of nine stocks. Nevertheless, through six months of Wave One testing, market participation shrank from 1,500 traders to 1,123. The low numbers remained a major concern, not because they meant less accuracy but because they reflected less interest.

Wave Two markets were opened to all retail employees, and began with instruction sessions on the fine points of trading. One-third of Wave Two markets were populist questions, intended to attract new investors and sustain interest among existing ones. Two-thirds involved Best Buy issues. One populist security asked how often CEO Brad Anderson would use the expression "lifestyle groups" during a conference call. The market wildly overestimated the number—perhaps a biased result, because Anderson was tipped about the question before his call.

A widely reported TagTrade success came in January 2008 with a Severts-inspired security to predict quarterly sales of a laptop computer–service package. A week before Best Buy launched the package, the prediction market estimate was 33 percent lower than the team's official sales forecast. On launch date it was 25 percent lower. Initial sales matched the pessimistic TagTrade prediction. The package was withdrawn and redesigned.

Eight months later, another TagTrade security was offered to gauge the chance of relaunching the new package on schedule. This launch-on-time share price suggested an 85 percent probability of being on time. Severts said he "took great comfort from that." The redesign was delivered on schedule.

Another TagTrade market asked participants whether they thought a new Best Buy store in Shanghai would open on schedule. Construction managers were saying yes. The TagTrade market, which included investors both at the head office and in Shanghai, said no. The price for an on-time opening dropped from $80 a share to $44. Here, as with other TagTrade markets, it was the rapid change in market numbers, more than absolute numbers, that generated e-mail alerts to management. The alert triggered by the rapidly falling Shanghai market resulted in extra resources being assigned to store completion. In spite of the move, the market was correct; the opening was delayed a month. Since then, TagTrade markets have run on all new Best Buy store openings and have continued to prove accurate.

The least successful TagTrade markets have involved attempts to predict sales of game modules. Ideally, the mid level of the market matches the sales estimate of the market forecast group. The market price should go no lower than 25 percent or higher than 75 percent because, at extreme ranges, traders would show a long-shot bias. However, the company's forecast group estimate was so far off that TagTrade results were of little use. This is another version of garbage-in, garbage-out. If you ask investors to choose a most-likely sales level within the wrong sales range, they will try, but the result will be garbage-out.

This failure highlights an obvious follow-up question: "If prediction markets generally produce more accurate forecasts and strategic answers, why have a group of highly paid forecasters at all?" The answer is that the forecasting group contributes to the prediction market by providing accurate prediction ranges. The solution may be to recognize and compensate the forecasting group based on the accuracy of the market.

Two kinds of home-team bias have been identified in TagTrade markets. As with Google markets, investors overpay for outcomes seen as favorable for the company. Securities on unfavorable outcomes are systematically undervalued. The second bias arises from an underestimation of a competitor's abilities, particularly those of Circuit City, Best Buy's then-major competitor. Because these biases are known, they can be taken into consideration in interpreting market results.

A potential source of TagTrade questions is a Best Buy electronic bulletin board, Blue Shirt Nation. Created in 2007 by two marketing employees and named for the outfits worn by sales staff, the board is where twenty-three thousand sales associates post questions and comments. If comments suggest a serious problem, one response is to list the issue as a TagTrade security and get broader input. The same sales associates provide customer service and answer questions through social media websites such as Twitter and Facebook. Associates learn what customers are concerned with—and use these insights to invest in TagTrade securities.

By mid-2011, TagTrade had run 240 prediction contracts. The participation problem persisted, with only 2,100 of the company's 115,000 US employees taking part in the market—500 of those from the head office. The low participation rate of store employees is related to their youth, their unfamiliarity with stock trading, and for many, their short tenure with the company. Not surprisingly, long-term employees are more likely to take part in the market.

There are different initiatives to keep existing investors in the TagTrade market and to attract new ones. Each trader starts a trading period with an account of $1 million. This is renewed each period even if she loses all of her money in the previous period. Each period, top investors receive a $200 gift certificate and an embroidered TagTrade shirt. The shirt seems to be at least as highly valued as the gift certificate. Traders get $25,000 in their account for each new investor they sign up who actually trades.

Some TagTrade investors complained that they could never win because they were not willing to devote as much time to the process as other employees. To keep them in the market, a gift card is awarded to participants who earn an additional $500,000 over the $1 million they started with, whether they are one of the top ten prize-winning investors or not. There is also a weekly draw for a gift certificate among those who have made at least one trade that week, whatever their results. There is a weekly motivational e-mail with updates about existing markets and new securities. The need for continuing motivation for non–prize winners was lesson five.

Unlike the Mutual Fun Market, no one at Best Buy monitors whether individual managers or employees take part. Severts said he is glad that Anderson encouraged participation but did not pressure reluctant managers to take part: "Nothing would squeeze the life out of TagTrade faster than putting it at the top of a priority list."

A market on whether the IT department would complete a systems upgrade on schedule motivated managers to expand TagTrade to investors outside the company. Much of the technical side of the upgrade was being carried out by three hundred specialists from consulting firm Accenture, who did not have access to the TagTrade market. So Best Buy did what no other large corporate prediction market has done: it opened Tag-Trade to suppliers. All Accenture personnel working on Best Buy projects were made eligible, and two hundred chose to take part. This is a much higher participation rate than Best Buy achieves, again reflecting the influence of education levels and previous stock-trading experience.

Accenture traders sign a confidentiality agreement, and a Best Buy legal team reviews what can be divulged to them. Accenture also offers its own questions on TagTrade. Accenture employees are not eligible for Best Buy prizes because this might strain the client-consultant relationship, or create dual loyalty. Instead Accenture provides prizes for its own employees. Tracking Accenture employee–produced predictions generates a heads-up to Accenture managers as well as to Best Buy. The next logical extension of TagTrade would be to allow customers to take part. However, Best Buy has thought it prudent to avoid potential problems with security regulators until the legal status of markets is resolved.

When TagTrade was first initiated, Circuit City was a competitive number two to Best Buy in the US electronics market. The companies had similar access to retail locations and suppliers. They had similar price policies and monitored each other's advertised prices. Through all of 2008, and particularly through that year's Christmas season, Circuit City posted dismal results. In January 2009, the company announced it would close its 567 stores and lay off 34,000 employees. At the time of the insolvency, Best Buy had $28 billion in US electronics sales, Walmart $17 billion (in electronics), and Circuit City $10.5 billion. But Walmart sold on a lowest-price appeal rather than on customer service, so Best Buy and Circuit City viewed each other as the major competitors.

The buzz around Best Buy's markets has credited TagTrade with insights that helped the company survive and prosper. This view may be more myth than fact, but it is interesting to look at how prediction markets might have helped save Circuit City. The most frequently cited mistake made by Circuit City management was the 2007 decision by CEO Philip Schoonover (who had four years earlier come to the company from Best Buy) to lay off thirty-four hundred of Circuit City's most experienced sales staff. This was part of Schoonover's attempt to lower costs by converting employees from a commission to a salary model. Those laid off were replaced with new hires, paid substantially less. Customers were exposed to a lot of negative media coverage about the layoffs and the perception that Circuit City would be offering a lower level of professional service. Circuit City employee morale suffered; employees' blogs said there was no longer any loyalty to the corporation, just to a particular store or department.

With its reduced service, Circuit City repositioned itself against price competitor Walmart. The problem was that Circuit City still charged higher prices than Walmart. Customers had come to both Best Buy and Circuit City for solutions to their questions on what gadget to buy and how to use it. Walmart sales associates could not provide those answers, nor could Amazon. With the repositioning of Circuit City, Best Buy strengthened its position as the prime destination for customers looking for informed buying advice plus the option of installation and service.

In the year before it failed, Circuit City's sales-floor employee turnover was 175 percent, compared with Best Buy's 50 percent. At the time of the insolvency, the average sales-floor employee at Best Buy had more than twice the tenure of his Circuit City counterpart. Best Buy's various social networking initiatives—including TagTrade and Blue Shirt Nation, and the culture of openness and trust that they encouraged—were credited with increasing employee involvement in the company.

Best Buy never considered running a prediction market on the impact of replacing experienced sales staff, or on the impact of Circuit City's doing so. Even exploring the issue would have created huge morale concerns among its longest-serving sales people.

Circuit City was also criticized for its emphasis on larger, more expensive flat-screen TVs and its focus on HD/DVD. Best Buy shifted emphasis to medium-screen TVs, smaller electronics such as iPods and game modules, and the Blu-Ray format. Several Best Buy prediction markets had helped Best Buy make decisions on these products, including a TagTrade market on Blu-Ray market share versus HD/DVD. The company wanted to know which of these two competing formats would prevail. It asked questions about market share. The TagTrade market was thought ideal for this; store employees were of the same age and demographic as their customers and exposed to a lot of information about the two formats. The market predicted an end-of-market Blu-Ray share of 77 percent. The actual end-of-market share was 74 percent. The predicted Blu-Ray shares were closer to actual numbers than those from any other research source. The TagTrade results fed into a Best Buy decision to drop the HD/DVD format and stock Blu-Ray products exclusively.

Another market asked how long an average customer would have to wait for at-home Geek Squad service during the month of January. The market, whose investors were mostly sales employees, estimated between five and six days. The business team's official forecast was four days. The actual time was 5.9 days. This market produced the result that every prediction market advocate dreams of: members of the forecasting team traded against their official forecast, emphasizing the power of anonymity in the market.

TagTrade flourished in large part because Severts adhered to his lesson number three, "From the beginning, air cover from top management is essential." It sounds like a good rule. Could a prediction market flourish if it had only token support from higher levels of the management hierarchy? The next chapter offers a case history of one market that did.

9

The Technology Evangelist

Some Oracle must rectify our knowledge.

—William Shakespeare, *The Tempest*, Act V, Scene 1

RITE-SOLUTIONS AND Google have had great success with their markets because of their company cultures, and because each market has the unquestioned support of top management. Could a prediction market succeed in a company with a more traditional hierarchical structure, or where top management offered only token support (probably the situation with the companies that most readers work with)? Could these impediments be overcome just by having a dedicated prediction market proponent driving the process? With the right person, such a market might flourish. Meet Misys Banking Systems. And meet Fortune Elkins, whose business card reads "Technology Evangelist."

Founded in 1979, Misys develops and licenses software for financial services and health-care companies worldwide. In the banking area—one of Misys's four divisions—the company services corporate treasury departments. By 2009 Misys had annual sales of about a billion dollars. The banking division has forty-five hundred employees, 40 percent of whom write computer code. Its customers include most of the world's top fifty banks. Misys is headquartered in the small English town of Evesham, about thirty miles from Birmingham, close to the Cotswolds. The Misys banking group has offices in New York City, London, Paris, Dubai, Hong Kong, Seoul, Frankfurt, Bangalore, and Bucharest.

Many Misys executives have English public-school backgrounds (in North America, this means private school), followed by a degree from Oxford or Cambridge. At one time, the company's best-known board member was Rupert Soames, grandson of Winston Churchill. Misys is a hierarchical pyramid organization with lots of boxes, the sort that Jim Lavoie disparages.

Because of its organizational structure and geographic and linguistic diversity, Misys was never an obvious candidate for a prediction market where junior code writers and receptionists would suggest tactics and strategy to Oxbridge-educated managers.

Fortune Elkins, then in her early forties, worked in the Treasury and Capital Markets unit of Misys's New York office. Her given name was inspired by Carl Orff's *Fortuna Imperatrix Mundi*, his setting of a medieval poem about how Fortune rules the world.

I met her at a prediction markets conference in San Francisco in early 2009. She described how she initiated and maintained prediction markets for the banking division of Misys, largely through the sheer force of her own personality. Elkins reflects another interesting aspect of prediction markets: a high proportion of them are started by women. She thinks this is because women are more accepting of the idea that social networks are a great way to share information and produce good decisions. The story of Misys and Fortune Elkins says a lot about how markets can be introduced, even in an unpromising work environment.

Elkins started at Misys in 2000, hired from AIG as a Web designer and information architect. In 2004, she read *The Wisdom of Crowds* and debated the usefulness of prediction markets with Ed Ho, the CEO of her division. Ho was interested, and Elkins's colleague Donal McGranaghan suggested that she prepare a formal presentation.

Elkins trolled Google for insights on how to construct a business case for a prediction market. She found the economic argument in articles by Justin Wolfers, Eric Zitzewitz, and Robin Hanson. Context on the organizational setting came from articles by psychologist Philip Tetlock and MIT's Tom Malone. She worked up a business case with a decision tree showing the huge value of improving information, plus a return-on-investment (ROI) calculation that suggested a prediction market would be a very profitable undertaking.

Elkins presented to Misys's Treasury and Capital Markets Board in January 2007. The questions that followed were those she had anticipated. Were employees motivated enough to learn to trade? Were they smart enough to make good trades? Could the market be manipulated? Would there just be casual day trading? These were easily answered from the literature on prediction markets. Finally, "Would the results be accurate?" To this she answered, "Why would I tie myself to a stake and set it on fire?" The board approved a trial market.

As had Jeff Severts at Best Buy, Elkins decided to lease Consensus Point prediction software rather than developing her own. The initial fixed cost and risk was lower than buy or build options, and there was no maintenance cost. The leasing option had a lower projected ROI than a software purchase, but that was offset by the lower risk. In two weeks, Elkins was up and running, with a new job description that included "corporate change and innovation, employee collaboration, and intelligent strategy."

First she sent out a mass e-mail for Ed Ho, explaining to employees what the market was about. Everyone was encouraged to invest—executives, product managers, code warriors, salespeople, and receptionists. *Especially* receptionists. Elkins says of Misys receptionists, "They see everything, schedule meetings, take messages, hear about problems. Everything passes through their inbox, confidential and not." This echoes Jim Lavoie's "Why would you not use all the available intellectual bandwidth?"

She ran training sessions on how to trade and in particular, how to sell short. The problem was that selling short was interpreted as investing against the company's success. Employees were incredibly reluctant to do that; it seemed disloyal. Suggesting her colleagues might sell short was akin to telling them it was OK to invest in the failure of a project that their company supported. Taking part in a market that might predict failure meant that employees were torn between supporting the team and their frustration at management's nonresponsiveness to other forms of communication. Elkins discovered that a market makes morale problems like these very visible. To promote short-selling, she explained to investors that they were not being disloyal, they were just providing Ed Ho the information he needed to do his job. Employees were anxious to communicate with management, and they understood the dilemma.

But the "selling short equals disloyalty" concern never really went away. One of Elkins's top ten traders told her that, after a while, she "just could not find it in herself to invest against Misys any more." This is a problem that bedevils every internal prediction market; company employees want to be team players, sometimes at the cost of not delivering bad news at an early stage. Elkins continually had to remind investors that short-selling is desirable, not disgraceful.

To ensure that every investor in every office could make decisions with the same information, she created the Misys Market Business Broadcasting Service. Twice a week she e-mailed one-page reports of market activity, product-related news updates, hiring updates, statements from product managers on the progress of projects, and trading strategies being followed by top-10 investors. This served to keep interest in the markets alive, improve liquidity, and squelch water-cooler gossip.

Of the Misys employees who signed up, 40 percent did so in the first five hours after the market was announced. Ultimately, 230 of 650 employees took part, an amazingly high percentage. Elkins allowed employees to trade under screen names; however, several product and project managers decided to express faith in their teams by taking the reputational risk of trading under their own names.

One of Elkins's first projects was the most dramatic imaginable. In early 2007, Misys got a new CEO. Mike Lawrie came to the position from Siebel and before that from a long career at IBM—both organizations with highly formalized planning and strategy procedures. One of Lawrie's first moves at Misys was to hire blue-chip consulting firm McKinsey to produce a three- to five-year strategy plan to improve the company's financial performance. He asked McKinsey whether Misys should focus on software for the financial sell side (investment banks) or the buy side (hedge funds, asset managers, pension funds, and private equity). If the answer was buy side, which user category would be most profitable?

Elkins ran prediction markets with questions that mimicked those asked of McKinsey. This was not a beauty contest predicting what others might say to McKinsey; it was structured as a series of "Where should Misys invest?" questions. McKinsey's final recommendations were the benchmark for the right answer. Most employees that McKinsey interviewed also chose to invest in the market. Not surprisingly, the market produced exactly the same answers as did the consulting group. The fee to lease Consensus Point software plus the cost of twenty prizes came to $5,500. That was the out-of-pocket cost for a prediction market that almost completely replicated the McKinsey assignment.

Over the next eighteen months, the Misys market offered seventy new questions, of which forty-two related to whether new products would launch on time. Others dealt with whether Misys sales revenue forecasts would be achieved in the United States and other countries. On all sales forecast questions, receptionists as a group were more successful investors than were engineers. Ed Ho listened to what the market said. Investors recognized that he listened, and kept investing.

New-product launch questions included, "Will project X be delivered by Y date?" or "Can the number of critical bugs in project X be reduced below Y number by Z date?" The bug question was important because of the tendency of software developers, facing a tight deadline, to deliver a bug-infested product and fix it later (or to rely on someone else to fix it). The majority of Misys prediction markets dealt with the core issues of the company's business model: can we do the project on time, can we do it right, and can we do it ahead of competitors?

Elkins also included questions that probably seemed frivolous but were intended to reveal employees' fears about the economic environment. "What is the highest rate of unemployment that will be registered prior to March 2010?" and "When will the recession end?" She found, as others have, that markets are addictive. Once she found a better way to predict, others contributed questions.

One of the early Misys contracts involved a product called Loan IQ; this was lending software that had been in development for more than a year. Loan IQ was notorious in the Misys Midtown, New York, office. Even the project manager rolled his eyes when the name was mentioned.

To reenergize the project, management appointed a new project manager, a woman with a strong history of on-time delivery. They also shuffled the software development team. Elkins opened a contract on whether Loan IQ would deliver on schedule. Almost all investors in the Midtown office promptly shorted the contract—the probability of on-time delivery was under 10 percent. In discussions with investors, Elkins discovered that not only did they not believe an outside project manager could deliver; they had little confidence in the whole project management process. Misys employees revealed both a "not invented here" mentality and an institutional morale problem.

The most successful investor in the Loan IQ market was a programmer in Misys's Pearl River, New York, office. Pearl River is on the New Jersey border; the office is sufficiently remote from the Manhattan office that most Pearl River programmers had never visited. The investor read the twice-weekly e-mail reports, relied on his own understanding of good software development, decided on-time completion was feasible, then invested heavily and drove up the price of the security that everyone else had shorted. When the project did complete on time, the Pearl River investor scooped the investment of most of the Midtown office. He catapulted to the top of the leader board and remained there for sixteen months. The product, called DataNet, is now a successful Misys module.

Misys markets proved to be 96 percent accurate as measured against actual outcomes, and were far more accurate than Misys's own internal three-month forecasts. Even with product-launch questions running for three months, the market usually produced the right answer in the first thirty to forty days. The challenge was to get management to pay attention and use the heads-up to assign new resources. The typical software-development contract carried a 10 percent penalty for missing a delivery target, so advance market information about not-on-time was valuable.

The grand prize in the pilot market was two round-trip tickets on Jet Blue to anywhere in the United States. Other than that introductory splurge, Misys prediction market prizes were Amazon.com gift cards for $75, $50, or $25—what Elkins called "the true global currency." There was also a worst-investor prize, as well as drawings for Misys coffee mugs. Ed Ho offered ego-stroking by recognizing successful investors at employee meetings and thanking others for taking part. Only three traders dropped out of the market during its first eighteen months of operation.

Offering anonymity also proved to be important. One reason traders stayed in is that they were allowed to use screen names. Like Jim Lavoie, Elkins thinks there are employees who will not speak up in meetings because they are junior, or intimidated, or introverts. They will contribute through investing if they can use a screen name.

Misys markets used play money, called Misys Moolah. Elkins relied on Moolah because she believed in the *endowment effect*—once market participants own play money, they treat it as seriously as if it were real. The amount each investor has accumulated is posted and determines status within the investor group. Elkins rewarded successful investors with millions in Moolah and reported how much each investor had accumulated on the leader board. The Amazon gift cards were awarded based on Moolah totals at the end of each market.

Elkins had two further goals. The first was to expand her internal market to other divisions of Misys. The second was to take the market external, to broaden the source of investors to include customers, user groups, and industry analysts.

In February 2009, the credit crisis hit Misys's banking division. Software orders remained strong but there was a wave of cost cutting, which included buying out many managers. One of the buy-outs was Fortune Elkins. After Elkins's departure from the company, a funny thing happened.

Even though no one was managing the Misys prediction market, it continued on its own. Many of the questions had an end of May 2009 termination. Two questions on the economy ran to the end of 2010. There were no newsletters, no updates, no promises of prizes or of management attention to predictions. But no investors dropped out. The Misys market had taken on a new life as a self-perpetuating networking site.

10

Boardroom Markets

If only HP knew what HP knows, we would be three times more productive.

     —Lew Platt, former CEO of Hewlett-Packard

A company that can predict the future is a company that is going to win.

     —Bernardo Huberman, Hewlett-Packard

RITE-SOLUTIONS, MISYS, and Best Buy are bottom-up prediction markets: questions originate at lower levels of the organizational pyramid, and market results flow upward. If a company wanted to use a prediction market on really major issues, could markets be initiated top-down, even from board level?

Lew Platt's quote, "If only HP knew what HP knows," became a mantra for supporters of markets. It was motivated by the most important top-down problem—the difficulty CEO Platt and his Hewlett-Packard board faced with signing off on decisions where the background information was too voluminous to process. Because of this volume, HP board members got to see summaries instead of source documents before signing off on decisions. This was true whether the agenda item was certification of financial statements, approval of a new product, or a proposed merger or joint venture.

A business unit or division of HP assembled information, summarized it, massaged it, and edited it. Information and recommendations got passed up the organization hierarchy. The material that reached the board was so many steps removed from operating-level wisdom that it was pretty hard to identify information gaps or biases.

When this multistep filtering process leads to problems, they are often major. In several recent corporate disasters, notably WorldCom and Enron, either the CEO controlled the information flowing to the board or individuals or groups at lower management levels were able to withhold corporate information from auditors and the board. If WorldCom's directors had timely information about how unsuccessful hundreds of its corporate acquisitions had been, or about the faulty accounting process that helped bring that company down, they might have found a solution. Had Enron's directors had a way to understand what Chief Financial Officer Andrew Fastow was doing with off-balance-sheet partnerships, they might have avoided that company's collapse.

Should the CEO or the board initiate prediction markets to assist with questions of interest to them, rather than just asking to see the status of markets already running? That does not sound like a profound query, but top-down markets have only occasionally been tried. Data from already-existing markets does reach board level, but for the most part it is information the board does not need to see.

Lew Platt's quote followed one of the earliest classic experiments with prediction markets, HP's attempt to forecast printer sales. The company's traditional process—staff specialists providing demand estimates and competitor analyses—had not produced very good results. HP executives decided to get predictions from their own sales force.

This was a promising idea; HP salespeople knew a lot about their customers and about the market. But HP faced the same problem as Best Buy. When salespeople were asked to forecast their own quarterly sales numbers, the quota-based commission and bonus system encouraged underestimates. HP understood this, and scaled up estimates by 20 percent to produce a "real" number as a basis for establishing production levels and advertising budgets. Salespeople quickly figured out what was happening, and further dropped their estimates to compensate. The forecasts were then really inaccurate, and on occasion led to inventory shortages.

HP retained Charles Plott, an economist from Caltech, to work with Kay-Yut Chen, a senior scientist at HP Labs, with a mandate to design and run a prediction market. In the late 1990s, Plott and Chen created a market where the same salespeople who had previously provided forecasts could trade in a market for sales projections.

About a quarter of HP's printer division people took part—salespeople, and also product and finance managers. Each began with twenty shares to invest in a prediction of total group printer sales at the end of the month. There were ten sales scenarios: less than 15,000 units sold; 15,000–16,000; 16,000–17,000; and so on. A trader who thought the company would sell 17,000–18,000 units could buy a contract for that amount. If her opinion changed, she could sell that contract and purchase another. She could also spread her investment over several contracts.

Each market ran for a week. The trading position at the end of a market was interpreted as the prediction of future sales. If the 15,000–16,000 level for December had 40 percent of the shares, that was interpreted as a 40 percent probability of December sales being in that range. When final sales figures were available, the company bought back shares in the winning contracts for $1 a share.

Market rewards were modest; the most a trader could win was $20 per week. Nevertheless, HP's prediction market results beat the company's formal forecasts in fifteen of sixteen periods when the two systems were run side-by-side. The average prediction market forecast was off 6 percent. Traditional forecasts were off an average of 13 percent, even after being revised upward.

The accuracy of the prediction market result was amazing, particularly given that HP allowed the market to run only at lunchtime and in the evening. It did not want salespeople to trade when they should be performing more traditional tasks—a loud signal to participants that the market might not be considered very important.

Sales projections for monthly printer sales were not important enough to reach the HP board, but the outcome of a subsequent HP prediction market experiment did. In 2006, Bernardo Huberman and Leslie Fine of HP's social computing lab began using markets to forecast the price of computer memory chips three and six months in advance. This was, and is, a critical issue for the company. Memory accounted for 12 percent of the manufacturing cost of an HP computer. A small error in estimating memory cost could wipe out quarterly profit. HP found that chip prices were easier to predict than printer-sales volumes.

In the first approach to forecasting price, a group of executives from the memory-chip division sat around a table, debated trends, and produced an estimate. In the second approach, the same executives presented arguments around the same table, but with no debate or rebuttal. They each then went to their own computers and invested in an online market. The second approach produced a 25 percent improvement in predicting memory-chip cost, even though the same people took part in both processes. The predictions were input into HP's purchasing, pricing, and marketing programs.

With this market, Huberman and Fine had the additional challenge of extracting a good result from a market with few participants. The solution was to have each investor answer a series of questions meant to evaluate their degree of risk aversion. Their investments were then combined with their risk index. Huberman and Fine concluded that good predictions could be generated from a market with fourteen investors. HP has patented the risk system, which it called BRAIN (for Behaviorally Robust Aggregation of Information in Networks).

The classic example of a board-motivated market was one British Petroleum (BP) set up in 1998 to forecast how best to reduce greenhouse gas emissions. BP chairman John Browne had made a sudden and unanticipated announcement that the company would proactively implement an ambitious emissions control policy. He promised that by 2010, BP would reduce its emissions to 90 percent of 1990 levels.

BP had 130 separate business units in more than 100 countries. Each business unit operated independently, and was evaluated on the basis of its profit contribution. The cost of reducing emissions varied across each unit and country. The problem was how to achieve the overall reduction target at the lowest cost.

The conventional approach was for senior managers to establish reduction targets for each business unit. Every unit would then insist its target was unreasonable, and several rounds of bargaining would follow. Those units that found it easy to reach their negotiated target would do so but have no incentive to go further. Others would spend great amounts of money to achieve their target or would give up.

John Mogford, the company's vice president for Health, Safety, and Environment, was entrusted with solving the problem. He first considered the traditional approach, imposing a solution from senior management. But Mogford knew from his own experience in BP that managers of individual business units knew the most efficient way to proceed—and that they had no incentive to pass this information up the hierarchy.

Mogford decided to establish an intranet-based market. Each business unit started with an allotment of annual carbon dioxide emissions. Business units could buy or sell this capacity, either in anticipation of future need or as a speculation. If one unit head saw an easy way to exceed his negotiated target, he could sell his extra capacity to other business units. Several units chose to shut down polluting production facilities when managers predicted that the unit was better off selling the now-unneeded emissions capacity.

The market facilitated emissions trading by revealing the transaction price that would allow worldwide BP pollution reduction at the lowest possible cost. The $40 per ton price for emission reduction that met the company's target was a third lower than the $60 per ton estimate provided to the board prior to establishment of the market. In 2001, BP's market traded 4.5 million tons of carbon dioxide emissions. BP met its reduction target later that year—nine years ahead of target.

One of the interested observers of the market was Margaret Mogford, wife of John and head of environment at British Gas Group. In 2000, Ms. Mogford was seconded to the UK Department for the Environment to become head of the Emissions Trading Group Secretariat. The internal

BP market design became the basis for the UK emissions trading plan. Two years after that, the UK design became the basis for the European Union emissions trading plan.

Where else could board-initiated markets have been helpful? In 2002 the board of The Boeing Company reviewed proposals for its planned 787 aircraft. There were hundreds of separate decisions requiring board approval, including the type of aircraft to produce, the subcontracting of sections of the aircraft to foreign factories, and whether to use lightweight but hard-to-fabricate composite materials for the 787 airframe. The board discussions revolved around technical topics, where most members had little expertise. The board would have benefited from independent input. Boeing did not run a prediction market on these questions, but someone else did.

In June 2007, Emile Servan-Schreiber's prediction site Bet2Give launched a market allowing investment on whether the first Dreamliner would be delivered by its mid-2008 deadline. Bet2Give was a real-money site, but charities received investors' winnings.

Servan-Schreiber's idea was to aggregate the wisdom of Boeing employees, contractors, and subcontractors to test the target 2008 delivery date. He thought the prediction market would help Boeing avoid the disaster that hit Europe's Airbus Industries when its A380 superjumbo airliner ran into a long list of production delays and was two years late in achieving its initial delivery.

The Bet2Give Boeing prediction market operated just like Fortune Elkins's Misys market for on-time delivery (see chapter 9). A share price of 55 cents meant investors thought there was a 55 percent chance of on-time delivery. The market was understandably volatile. Many marginal traders sat back and waited for price swings, buying at 25 cents when a subcontractor snafu threatened to derail the project, then selling at 65 cents when the price went up following an enthusiastic, "We are on track!" pronouncement by a Boeing executive.

As scheduled delivery dates got closer, the on-time price stayed below 45 cents. By October 2007, four months before a formal announcement that the delivery date would be missed, the price had dropped to 24 cents.

The falling price could no longer be ignored. In December 2007, Boeing allocated $2 million in additional R&D money to the project and sent hundreds of its own employees to South Carolina, Italy, and Japan to assist contractors.

The extra resources came too late. In January 2008, Boeing mechanics in Seattle opened the first crates of fuselage sections intended for assembly. They found piles of brackets, clips, and wires that should have been preinstalled, but had just been tossed into boxes. Some components came with assembly documentation in Italian, some with no instructions at all.

In February 2008, Boeing announced a delay to late 2008 for delivery of the first 787. In July, they said that the delay would be a further six months. In September, the first delivery was rescheduled for late 2010. A Boeing spokesperson revealed that the company would be liable for a billion dollars in compensation payments and would incur a short-term loss on the 787 program. The first 787 was delivered to All Nippon Airways in September 2011, and entered commercial service a month later.

Boeing chairman and CEO James McNerney said he was amazed to learn of a lack of documentation on the work remaining to complete the first 787. He added that he was replacing Scott Carson, president of Boeing's Commercial Airplanes division, because Carson had not understood the scope of the problem. McNerney said, "You need insight into what's actually going on in those factories . . . had we had adequate insight, we could have helped our suppliers understand the challenges." McNerney's statement reflected how much more information Bet2Give investors appeared to have. Servan-Schreiber would probably have said that employees, suppliers, and customers had volunteered that information.

McNerney's experience of being blindsided by a project failure is sufficiently common that it became the subject of one of the all-time most-reproduced *Dilbert* cartoons. In the first frame, Wally wanders over to Dilbert's cubicle and asks, "How's your project coming along?" In frame two, Dilbert responds, "It's a steaming pile of failure. It's like fifteen drunken monkeys with a jigsaw puzzle." In the third panel, the pointy-haired boss wanders by a few minutes later and asks Dilbert, "How's your project coming along?" Dilbert responds, without looking up from his computer, "Fine."

Boeing has implemented an internal prediction market for its most recent project, the 581 passenger-stretch version of the 747. Designed to challenge the Airbus A380, it was designated the 747–81. The aircraft had its first public showing in June 2011 at the Paris Air Show. The prediction market, run by a commercial partner in California, started in spring 2011 and will monitor completion metrics for the new aircraft.

BP is another firm that would have benefited from a prediction market. Other than its top-down emissions pricing experiment, BP has not made use of the collective wisdom of its employees and partners. The company has been prone to unanticipated but very costly accidents. In 2005, an explosion at a Texas refinery killed fifteen BP workers. In 2006, an equally unanticipated rupturing of a corroded Alaska pipeline caused a huge oil spill in Prudhoe Bay.

Then on April 20, 2010, the BP *Deepwater Horizon* oil rig exploded, killing workers on the rig and spilling millions of barrels of crude oil into the Gulf of Mexico. The oil slick was 130 miles long and 75 miles wide and devastated the wetlands, coastal waters, and bayous of Louisiana, Alabama, Mississippi, and Florida. The resulting liability caused the value of BP stock to decline $40 billion over three weeks (from an original market value of $75 billion), and was so large that some analysts predicted the eventual breakup of the company.

BP had wildly underestimated the likelihood of each of these events. Nassim Nicholas Taleb has termed these *black swan events*, referring to the widely held belief, before 1697, that all swans were white. The sighting of the first black swan in Australia in that year is cited by Taleb as an example of the outlier, the event outside the realm of normal expectations. As with the swans, most individuals discount the likelihood of events that are difficult to imagine—the existence of the swan or the failure of an elaborately engineered blowout valve.

Conversely, we overestimate the probability of unlikely events that are easy to imagine. After 9/11, hundreds of thousands of Americans chose to drive rather than risk flying. There were no terrorist attacks on aircraft in the United States during 2002; those who drove were about fifteen times as likely to die per mile traveled as they would be flying.

Would a prediction market instituted after the refinery fire or oil pipeline leak have helped BP anticipate *Deepwater*? Probably, and especially if the market had included participants from BP subcontractors Transocean, Halliburton, and Cameron International who had detailed knowledge of the drilling and a different risk perspective to that of BP employees. Would a market on the risks of driving versus flying have caused more people to fly than drive in 2002? It is doubtful many would have paid attention.

In the *Deepwater* case, as in most project failures, someone (or a lot of someones) may know in advance about impending difficulty. The challenge is to get the someones to disclose—or to invest in—their beliefs.

How about a board of directors that is considering divesting one of its business units? There was spirited competition to acquire General Motor's European carmaker Opel following GM's 2009 insolvency. Could markets have been used to assist the GM board in estimating the value of selling a controlling interest to Canadian firm Magna International and its Russian partner Sberbank, rather than to Fiat or to Belgian private equity firm RHJ International?

This was a complicated issue, not only because each acquirer was bidding for a different combination of assets, but also because there were underlying political risks. German chancellor Angela Merkel and Russian president Dmitry Medvedev each viewed Fiat as likely to close German assembly plants, and viewed RHJ as a vulture investor. Each leader backed the Magna bid in the press.

How each government would respond to a Fiat or RHJ purchase was unclear. Would they support the new entity, guarantee loans to the acquirer, or commit to future purchases from GM if Opel were sold to anyone but Magna? The Merkel government said that if the Magna bid was not successful, Germany expected GM to immediately repay an outstanding €1.5 billion ($2.2 billion) state loan.

Two simultaneous markets might have provided an estimate of the value to GM's stakeholders of accepting one offer over the other. One market could ask for the value of GM stock in sixty days if the Magna offer were accepted and the other offers rejected. A second market could ask the value if the RHJ offer were accepted and the Magna offer rejected. Investments for the rejected bidder would be returned. After a long negotiating process, the GM board announced it would accept the Magna/Sberbank offer. Three weeks later, the board reversed the decision, canceled the sale, and said GM would retain the Opel division. The German government then requested repayment of the state loan.

Think of the length and detail of the process that leads to a board signing off on audited financial statements each quarter. Multinational conglomerate General Electric issues financial statements based on the aggregated results of more than a hundred business units doing business in 140 countries.

Many audit committees consist entirely of independent directors (not officers of the company). Board members are privy only to the information provided by management. Perhaps a board would be helped by a market that asks whether the firm will have to restate its financial statements within a year. This could be paired with a second market asking a contingent question, whether a subsequent investigation into financial reporting would find wrongdoing.

This is far from hypothetical. In August 2009, the US Securities and Exchange Commission fined GE $50 million (reportedly a quarter of the $200 million the company paid in accounting and legal fees to contest the matter) for "twisting accounting rules beyond the breaking point." The claim was that on four occasions in 2002 and 2003 and in order to meet analysts' expectations, GE shifted earnings that should have been recorded in a future period to a current accounting period. One violation involved recording revenue for locomotive sales that had not yet been finalized.

There was never any suggestion that any board member, or CEO Jeffrey Immelt, had prior knowledge of the income shifting. But some people at lower levels of the hierarchy certainly knew. Markets on restating earnings and the outcome of any subsequent investigation would have provided a measure of the completeness of the financial statements. Would employees invest truthfully in such a potentially damaging question? They might, if they believed it helped their company—and if they were sure of remaining anonymous. Results from the market could be made available to creditors and shareholders and might prove to be a more effective reassurance than tightening auditing and internal controls.

Prediction markets might also play a role in the long-existing debate about how a board should act when there is a takeover offer for the firm. With either a friendly or hostile offer on the table, board members receive only information from the CEO. Most board members will have had little experience in gauging the value of their company to an acquiring firm or, in the case of an exchange of shares, the projected earnings of the merged company. Information provided by shareholders, speculators, and arbitrageurs is helpful, but each source includes a large component of self-interest.

On February 1, 2008, Microsoft made an offer to the Yahoo! board to acquire all the outstanding common stock of that company for $31 a share. The offer was later raised to $33. The first price represented a 62 percent premium over the closing price of Yahoo! common stock the day before the offer. The second price was a 70 percent premium. Each offer was rejected by the Yahoo! board. The company's stock immediately dropped to $18 a share, and dropped as low as $12.80 during the year following.

The Microsoft offer could have been submitted to a market that asked the value of a Yahoo! share six months or a year later, contingent on the Microsoft offer not being accepted. If the prediction market value were higher than the offer, the board would have support in asking for more money. There would then be justification for thinking a third party might come forward with a better offer. If the prediction market value were lower than the Microsoft offer price, the board would have strong support for recommending acceptance.

The interesting footnote to these examples is that GM, GE, Microsoft, and Yahoo! (but not Boeing) each had some experience with internal prediction markets at the time of these events.

What would be the most important imaginable board-mandated market? The answer is suggested by Jim Collins's 2009 book *How the Mighty Fall . . . and Why Some Companies Never Give In.* Collins had led a discussion with a group composed of US Army generals, CEOs, and social-sector leaders at West Point Military Academy. The topic was whether America was renewing its greatness or was instead close to losing its past preeminence. One CEO posed a version of the same question, "When you are the most successful company in your industry, how would you know if your power and success might cover up the fact that you were already on the path to decline?" That question was the motivation for Collins's book.

Collins concludes that institutional decline is like a disease: harder to detect but easier to cure in the early stages; easier to detect but harder to cure in later stages. A corporation can appear strong even while on the cusp of a precipitous fall. He named as recent examples Xerox, HP, IBM, Nucor, Merck, Delta Air Lines, Disney, and Boeing.

Collins describes five stages in the decline of these and other corporations. Stage one is "Hubris born of success." Management becomes insulated by early success, and executives regard success as an entitlement. Stage two is "The undisciplined pursuit of more scale, more growth, more profit." Stage three is "Denial of risk and peril." Here warning signs mount, but are explained away as a product of uncontrollable external factors or a cyclical market. In this stage the CEO and board discount negative data, spin ambiguous data, and emphasize positive data.

At stage four, "Grasping for salvation," the cumulative damage from stage three throws the business into decline. Collins concludes that an enterprise does not visibly fail until stage four. The key to avoiding stage four is to take remedial steps in stage three. But in stage three, the CEO and board are still comfortable that everything is great. How can they monitor whether their interpretation of the health of the business is shared by others? Think of a regular series of prediction markets that asked straightforward questions: "What will be the company's share of market at the end of this quarter and next?" "What will be the company's stock price at the end of this quarter and the next?"

As an example of stage three malaise, consider investment bankers Bear Stearns. That company's stock peaked in 2007 at $172. The board, which apparently had no idea of how little the company's mortgage-backed bonds and derivatives were worth, approved almost $100 million in total 2006 compensation for CEO James Cayne and his copresidents Warren Spector and Alan Schwartz. Just before the stock peaked, a mathematician at Bear devised a risk-assessment matrix to value the firm's exposure to its investment portfolio. The risk prognosis was dire. Many senior executives apparently knew of the analysis and agreed with the conclusion. Cayne dismissed both the assessment and the methodology, and did not pass on the study to the board. Would a board-mandated prediction market have aggregated those fears to provide a heads-up? In early 2008, Bear Stearns went through a very quick stage four. JP Morgan purchased the wreckage of the investment firm for $2 a share. The price was later bumped to $10.

Toyota Motor Corporation is an example of a company that has reached stage four; at least, that is what president Akio Toyoda told an audience of Japanese journalists in October 2009. Toyota, he said, had already passed through Collins's description of "denial of risk and peril" and was well into "grasping for salvation." In the year before his talk, Toyota lost $4.1 billion—twice as much as General Motors lost over the same period—and saw its market share fall in every market. In the fourth quarter of 2011, Toyota was passed for the top global sales spot by both General Motors and Volkswagen AG.

It might have been useful to test Toyoda's stage-four conclusion through a prediction market. As far as I have been able to determine, no Japanese corporation has ever run one. (Several Japanese universities run highly publicized political prediction markets.)

Collins's stage five is capitulation to irrelevance or death.

If another argument is needed for a board-initiated market, it is found with the conclusions from Caltech professor Scott E. Page, who observed that, when faced with solving a problem or making a prediction, a diverse group is likely to yield a better result than a homogeneous group. What is the solution if there is not enough diversity in the boardroom? In

2010, women and all minorities represented 17.1 percent of board seats in *Fortune* 500 companies. African Americans alone, male and female, comprised 13 percent of the US population, but occupied 8.7 percent of board seats. Asians accounted for 3.5 percent, Hispanics 2.5 percent. If a company does not have diversity within its board of directors, perhaps the board should seek input from a prediction market composed of a more diverse set of investors.

PART THREE

Where Can Markets Take Us?

11

Way-Outside-the-Box Markets

Casting Calls and Epidemiology

That rainbow song is no good. Take it out.

—MGM memo criticizing the first cut of the movie *The Wizard of Oz*, 1938

There will be one million cases of AIDS in Britain by 1991.

—World Health Organization 1989 report on the AIDS outbreak [actual 1991 count: 7,699]

THE PREDICTION MARKETS described in previous chapters reflect straightforward, in-the-box thinking; all that is required is application of the premise, "None of us is as smart as all of us." But as with Google's tracking of the Evanston tribe (chapter 7), there are applications that move outside the box, and might never have occurred to even an avid proponent of markets. These include casting a musical comedy, tracking epidemics, assessing the success of a program to raise reading scores of sixth-grade students, and selecting players for a renowned football team. Each is presented with the hope it may suggest to the reader even more creative applications.

How about casting a major stage production using a televised prediction exercise? In 2006, composer Andrew Lloyd Webber, creator of *The Phantom of the Opera, Jesus Christ Superstar,* and *Evita,* among others, used a London television audience in a multiweek talent series, *How Do You Solve a Problem Like Maria?* The goal was to identify the ideal Maria von Trapp to star in Lloyd Webber's production of Rogers and Hammerstein's classic *The Sound of Music* in London's West End.

Lloyd Webber had first invited movie actor Scarlett Johansson to play the lead. This is a long-established way for a producer to create publicity and boost advance ticket sales: cast a celebrity and publicize the signing. But Johansson did not want to commit to live theater for a year when her movie career was taking off.

Using a television audience to judge talent had a previous and better-known application—the Fox TV hit *American Idol.* This singing competition allows viewers to vote by text message or telephone on the best singers and rockers. But *Idol* asks who viewers like most. The *Sound of Music* producers did not ask audiences to choose the best performer. Early in the program, Lloyd Webber described what audiences should look for: a woman who looked close in age to the eldest von Trapp daughter, could portray the innocence that characterizes Maria, and had a voice to fill a sixteen-hundred-seat theater. The role of Maria Augusta Rainer von Trapp, made famous by Mary Martin on stage and Julie Andrews on the screen, has been called the "biggest job on stage."

Fifty candidates were chosen from three hundred who responded to an audition call. Thirty of the fifty had serious experience in musical comedy. Each week, a studio and television audience viewed several performances and voted off the candidates who were thought furthest from Lloyd Webber's criteria. The voting process mimicked a prediction market. Each television viewer had up to six votes each week, through separate telephone calls. Since each call cost about £1 ($1.50), the casual viewer did not vote. Interested viewers might invest £1 each week in casting a single vote for their favorite. Avid supporters who voted six times invested £6 ($9). The reward was the satisfaction of having their favorite candidate survive the cut to perform the following week.

Lloyd Webber was allowed to save one performer a week, despite a low audience ranking. But the final choice of who would ultimately make or break a £10 million ($15 million) stage production was left to an amateur prediction group. Probably half of those voting had never seen a live London West End musical. But the television program was one of the highest rated in BBC history, with 2.25 million votes cast following the final sing-off. The program won an international Emmy award.

The London prediction exercise chose Connie Fisher, a complete unknown who had never performed outside of drama-school classes. Fisher's mother gave a newspaper interview where she criticized her daughter for giving up a steady job in retail to pursue the audition, because "she has little talent." The show opened at the London Palladium, and Fisher went on to win London's Critics' Circle Theater award for her portrayal of Maria. The show had the largest advance ticket sale in London theater history. Most of Fisher's performances sold out. Several of the unsuccessful contestants accepted roles in the production as nuns of Nonnberg Abbey.

The same prediction process was used to cast Maria in the Toronto production; the winner, Elicia Mackenzie, was also unknown and relatively inexperienced. Mackenzie's success in the role equaled Connie Fisher's.

Could prediction markets be used in another out-of-the-box way, to help limit the spread of AIDS? A recent and fascinating book, *The Wisdom of Whores* by Elizabeth Pisani, suggests that prostitutes could have told us a lot about the way AIDS spreads. The book discusses the experiences of sex workers around the world and the street smarts that stem from that experience.

Pisani is a journalist turned epidemiologist who worked for international health organizations in several countries. She concludes that the international response to AIDS has been wrongheaded. This view is supported by other critics, notably Canadian Stephen Lewis, former UN envoy on AIDS in Africa. The bureaucratic assumption was that AIDS is a pandemic that moves through a population. Pisani claims that everywhere but Africa, AIDS appears as a series of mini-epidemics among three high-risk groups: sex workers, drug injectors, and men having sex with men. She argues that spending on preventive resources for the entire population is wasteful when the risk for most people of contracting AIDS is minuscule. The extreme example is East Timor, which upon independence in 1999 received $2 million from the United States for a nationwide AIDS program. At the time, East Timor had seven known HIV-positive residents, all enrolled in drug-treatment programs.

Pisani concludes that the most cost-effective method of limiting AIDS transmission is the free distribution of clean needles, methadone, and condoms. Several people, in praising her book, pointed out that a prediction exercise involving experienced third-world sex workers might have reached this conclusion much earlier.

Another proposed health-care application combines a prediction market with a pay-for-performance vaccination project. What if an aid agency such as the Bill and Melinda Gates Foundation agreed to pay $15 for every child in Malawi vaccinated against malaria? A prediction market is used to estimate the number of children who would contract malaria in the absence of the $15 subsidy, as opposed to the number that would contract the disease if the subsidy were offered. These numbers provide the Gates Foundation with a market-based estimate of the benefit from offering the payment.

The Foundation then auctions the right to provide the vaccinations. Whoever offers the highest buy-in fee gets to vaccinate and receives the subsidy. Potential bidders base their bids on market estimates.

Offering the highest buy-in fee means that the successful bidder provides vaccinations at the lowest net cost to the Foundation. The bidder offers a lump sum, say $10,000, for the right to vaccinate, and receives $15 for each child vaccinated, once the number is confirmed by a third-party auditor. The cost to the Foundation is $15 times the number of inoculations, less the $10,000 fee. The bidder now has an economic incentive to locate and vaccinate children; each child above a breakeven number, say three thousand in this example, is highly profitable. The prediction market provides the Foundation with three numbers it did not have before: benefits from the vaccination program, net benefits, and the total cost to the Foundation. These estimates will be imperfect, but given what we know about markets, they will be better than what any other source might offer.

How about using markets in other forms of disease control—the flu in the American Midwest? In 2004, the Iowa Electronic Markets launched markets to predict influenza outbreaks. The previous year, infectious disease physician Phil Polgreen was at a party in downtown Iowa City, close to the Airliner Pub where the IEM was first conceived. Polgreen was introduced to the IEM's Forrest Nelson and George Neumann, and they started talking about the then-current epidemic of SARS. The disease posed a classic prediction problem: there was a lot of information available, but it was dispersed among many different people around the world. No one knew where the disease was spreading, or whether it would remain as a persistent health problem. Polgreen, Nelson, and Neumann talked about starting a SARS prediction market. Before they could act, the disease disappeared. They decided to open a flu market instead.

Influenza is an important health problem. From 5 to 20 percent of the US population contracts the flu each year, resulting in 36,000 deaths a year (there are 500,000 worldwide). Isolated outbreaks can quickly become local epidemics. It is important to identify outbreaks quickly to reposition vaccines, antiviral drugs, and specialists. Conventional infectious disease surveillance methods are quant-based but slow; they rely on analysis of current and historical data.

Conventional wisdom at the Centers for Disease Control (CDC) in Atlanta was that influenza was inherently unpredictable, sufficiently random that there was no way to predict future outcomes. Polgreen said one of his goals was to change the way the CDC and others thought about aggregating information. The reality was that medical professionals had information about outbreaks and trends and were willing to assist in prediction, but had no easy way to do so.

The Iowa flu market was set up to collect and report information fast enough to be clinically useful. Each Friday during the flu season, investors chose whether flu activity for the coming week in their state should be categorized in one of five groupings used by the CDC: no activity, sporadic, local, regional, or widespread. An early investor was Stacy Coffman, a microbiologist at the University of Iowa hospital. As an infection control professional, she is one of the first in the hospital to learn of local outbreaks. During the first season the market operated, she doubled her "flu buck" money. At the end of the flu season, Coffman received an education grant equal to the dollar value of flu bucks in her account.

The market assumes that family physicians, emergency room staff, pharmacists, and clinical microbiologists will be the first to observe any new outbreak or unexpected change in normal seasonal trends. These health-care workers invest online during their coffee breaks, instead of waiting until later to fill out and mail a report to the CDC. One early concern was that a flu vaccine producer would have a financial incentive to inflate predictions for incidence of illness in order to sell more vaccine at higher prices. There is no indication of this ever happening.

The market accurately predicted the outset, peak, and end of the influenza season two to four weeks ahead of CDC reports on flu activity. It also helped explain how geographic movement took place. Kids get the flu; parents stay home with the kids and they catch it. Parents carry the virus to their workplace and pass it to other parents, who take it home to their kids. The kids form most of the epidemic; adults are carriers and determine the geographic spread. The IEM predicted the level of severity during a coming week 85 percent of the time. Even when it missed a forecast, the market was never out by more than one level of severity on a five-level system.

A separate market predicts effectiveness of the current year's flu vaccine. Each year, the flu virus undergoes what is called antigenic drift; the vaccine must be reformulated annually so it matches the dominant strain of flu circulating in the population. If a vaccine mismatch occurs, illness and death from influenza increases dramatically. Information about vaccine effectiveness is normally available only at the end of the flu season. Earlier warning of a mismatch helps the medical community to prepare. Investment in the effectiveness market has come primarily from medical professionals who work with US military personnel, all of whom undergo compulsory vaccination.

FIGURE 11-1

Actual US flu activity, mid-Atlantic region, and Google Flu Trends predictions

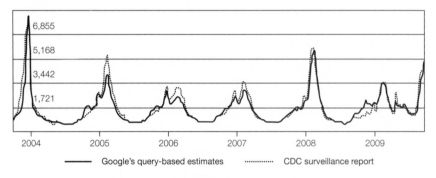

Source: Chart and data compliments of Google Flu Trends Project, 2009.

The Iowa flu market has been partly superseded by the Google flu market, part of the widely used Google Trends. Many Americans who are feeling unwell enter Google search phrases like "flu symptoms" even before calling their doctors. Related search words like "thermometer," "muscle ache," and "chest congestion" are also counted, but are assigned a lower weight. This flood of inquiries has been turned into the Google Flu Trends prediction system, which can spot fast-developing outbreaks. Google shows where outbreaks are occurring and the direction in which the flu is spreading (see figure 11-1).

The graph shows six years of query-based flu estimates for the mid-Atlantic region of the United States (the solid line) compared with flu surveillance data collected later and publicized by the CDC's FluView/Influenza Surveillance Report (the broken, more jagged line). Estimates based on Google search queries match every change in the incidence of flu. Flu Trends identifies influenza outbreaks a week to ten days before they are reported by the CDC.

In theory, Trends could be used to chart almost any medical phenomenon from allergy attacks to a potential pandemic. The Trends system is available in Chinese as well as in English. Researchers are investigating whether data from Google's Chinese site can be used to predict the transmission of infectious diseases from animals and birds to humans.

In chapter 7, I discussed the use of cell phone signals to track the movement of individuals to learn their favorite restaurants and nightclubs. Sense Networks proposes to use the same technology in the health sector, initially to model and predict the spread of HIV and tuberculosis in South Africa. Citysense will track the movements of infected patients being treated at Helen Joseph Hospital in Johannesburg. Upon release from the hospital, each patient will be asked to carry a mobile phone and leave it turned on. This will reveal how patients commute and what neighborhoods they visit. Understanding patterns of travel by infected patients, and inferring they travelled the same routes before they became infected, will help identify where authorities should concentrate the search for new infections.

There are many other things that could be revealed by involuntary markets. Google's Hal Varian did a study in 2009 showing that peaks and troughs in the volume of Google searches for products such as cars and vacations predicted shifts in sales of those products three to seven days later. Changes in Google searches for job-related terms are a good predictor of changes announced in the next release of US employment statistics.

The same prediction market–based, pay-for-performance idea suggested for vaccinations could be applied to education. Robert Hahn, director of the American Enterprise Institute–Brookings Joint Center for Regulatory Studies in Washington, DC, envisions the following scenario: There is a school district that needs to improve sixth-grade reading scores by ten points. The school creates a prediction market that asks how much test scores will change over a three-month period if a private contractor is hired to mentor students and paid on the basis of improved scores. Teachers, parents, and anyone else with an interest in the subject can invest. The school district uses the information to decide whether to go ahead with the program. If it does, potential bidders use the results to help decide whether to buy into the program and how much to invest.

If the school district proceeds, the right to offer the reading-improvement program is awarded to the highest bidder. The winner pays a lump sum. The mentoring organization then receives, say, $50 for each point of reading improvement for each sixth-grader over the three-month period. The bidder gets paid for what it delivers. If test scores go up, the school board pays. If they don't, the contractor is out both the fee and the cost of the program.

The market could be tweaked by asking a sequence of questions: How much would the average test scores of children from low-income families go up? How would the scores of middle-class children be affected? Greater payment-per-point could be offered for improvement in sixth graders from low-income areas.

A two-market approach to the same problem comes from John Ledyard at Caltech. The first market pays $10 if reading scores increase 10 points over six months, conditional on a private-tutor company not being hired. If the company is hired, investors get their money back. The second asks about reading scores increasing, conditional on a private-tutor company being hired. If the company is not hired, investors get their money back.

The contract describes what the company is allowed to do to raise scores. The market provides a prediction outcome and a basis for deciding how much to pay the private-tutor company to offer the program. Markets could be run with the same question but with different options as to what the tutor is allowed to do.

In chapter 3, I showed how prediction markets are incredibly accurate at predicting the outcome of sporting events. Could you also use a market not to predict the outcome of a match, but to select the strategy used to run a team? Spanish football club Real Madrid Club de Fútbol, known as Real Madrid and owned by club members, certainly comes close.

Socios abonados, the fifty-eight thousand Real Madrid members who pay dues and also hold season tickets, get to elect the club president every four years. Their evolving preferences between the four-year presidential voting periods, which the club monitors, measure how the club is doing and what it should do. Members express views on raising season ticket prices (most years the club does not), what sponsor names appear on team shirts, and how prominent such logos should be. This is a market, not a poll. Those who don't care don't register a preference. Those who do care register a strong preference. Extended families often conspire to cast multiple votes.

For years, members have cast their votes in favor of the competition model the club should follow, in a system not used by any other football club in the world. The Real Madrid model involves bringing in five superstar foreign players, whom the club calls *galacticos*, to match with six Spanish players. Past Real players Zinedine Zidane, Ronaldo, Luis Figo, and David Beckham were responses to this *socios abonados*–mandated model. The captain must always be one of the Spaniards. Real Madrid presidential candidates campaign not on the model—which is accepted as sacred—but on what players a candidate promises to add to the contingent of foreigners.

The transfer of Figo from rival club FC Barcelona was a key part of Florentino Pérez's July 2000 campaign for president. In 2009, returning to the club and again, Pérez wooed votes by promising to attract Kaká from Milan and Cristiano Ronaldo from Manchester United. It was an expensive promise; the two transfers were completed but cost Real £136 million (about $262 million).

Does a fan-mandated approach to structuring a team work? For the last decade, Real Madrid has been the most successful team in Spanish football. It was voted by FIFA, the world football federation, as the most successful club team of the twentieth century. Real Madrid has won a record thirty-one La Liga titles, seventeen Spanish Cups, nine European Cups, and two UEFA Cups. In 2010, it generated the highest revenue of any football team in the world, €460 million ($560 million), and was second in the football world in terms of team value and operating income, behind England's privately owned Manchester United.

As prediction markets applications move outside the box, some dramatic results occur. Ever-further-outside applications are suggested. How about using markets to predict terrorist attacks? The next chapter details the history of the US government doing just that.

12

Further Outside the Box
Terrorism Markets

In the case of 9/11 there was lots of valuable and relevant information available before the attack took place. What was missing was a mechanism for aggregating that information in a single place. A well-designed market might have served as that mechanism.

— James Surowiecki, in *Slate* Magazine

The difficulty lies not so much in developing new ideas as in escaping from old ones.

— John Maynard Keynes, British economist

WHEN TOM RIDGE BECAME US Secretary of Homeland Security in 2003, he said that innovation and new ideas must be a cornerstone of the fight against terrorism. One of Ridge's priorities was "encouraging new projects and innovations from entrepreneurs." Senator Ron Wyden of Oregon jumped on the security bandwagon and called for "a technology road map to strengthen our capacity to fight terrorism," adding that "a new generation of technologies and technology experts must be cultivated to meet future threats."

The mandate to create this technology road map was given to a blue-sky research arm of the US Department of Defense, the Defense Advanced

Research Project Agency, otherwise known as the mad-scientist wing of the Pentagon. DARPA was established at the height of the Cold War, in the dark days following the Soviet Union's 1958 *Sputnik* satellite launch. The agency was intended to bridge the gap between basic science and its military applications.

DARPA's history includes spectacular successes and a couple of famous flops. Its best-known accomplishment occurred in 1969, when agency researchers connected four computers to form ARPNET. This became a network linking the military, universities, and think tanks, and evolved to become the Internet. The agency funded development of the computer operating system UNIX and created the stealth technology used in military aircraft design. DARPA enjoyed less success with the prototype of a huge mechanical elephant designed to transport soldiers through Vietnam's jungles. It is now reported to be working on Cinder (for Cyber Insider Threat), software designed to guard against the escape of sensitive information—to stop a future WikiLeaks.

DARPA responded to its antiterrorism assignment with an innovative idea about how prediction markets might be used. The agency set up the Policy Analysis Market (PAM), a market solution to assess the threat of terrorism by aggregating information from sixteen separate US intelligence agencies that did not always cooperate with each other. They did not routinely share databases, so material collected by one organization did not automatically reach the others.

From Pearl Harbor to Korea to 9/11 to the attempted Christmas Day 2009 bombing of an airliner over Detroit, one or more intelligence agencies had some relevant information before the event. Four months prior to the attacks on the World Trade Center and the Pentagon, the FBI's New York field office was warned of the "inordinate number of individuals of investigative interest" seeking flight training in Arizona. That information was not passed on to the CIA. The US 9/11 Commission cited this and other examples of lack of sharing as "the biggest impediment to all-source analysis."

It was thought that a prediction market could produce consensus estimates without danger of revealing individual sources, and that government or intelligence agency employees who were under professional pressure to conform could report their real views anonymously to the market. The first PAM market was to trade securities on economic, civil, and military stability in Egypt, Jordan, Iran, Iraq, Israel, Saudi Arabia, Syria, and Turkey. These were to be one-year prediction markets, with contracts issued quarterly.

For each country, there were to be five securities on military activity, political instability, economic growth, and military and economic involvement with the United States. The political instability measure would track things like the frequency of large-scale demonstrations, political arrests, and unemployment levels. Later contracts were to involve predictions on global trade levels, deaths from terrorist attacks, and US military deaths from overseas duty. PAM was to start in September 2003 with one hundred investors, go to a thousand by November, and expand to a maximum of ten thousand investors by January 2004.

The Economist Intelligence Unit (part of the *Economist* magazine family) would conduct PAM's data analysis. Because trader anonymity was important, an offshore bank in a jurisdiction with bank secrecy, probably Lichtenstein, would hold PAM trader funds and pay out successful predictions. The bank would be the only entity to know the identity of PAM traders.

DARPA recognized that there was a circularity problem associated with markets on terrorism. If the CIA were to act on a market prediction that the Iraqi prime minister was at increased risk from an al-Qaeda assassination attempt, military and civilian security around him would be increased. This might deter the assassination attempt, but also invalidate investors' predictions.

This circularity problem is created by the way the security is worded. DARPA's response was to propose a contract not on assassination, but on whether the security force around the prime minister would increase by at least 50 percent at any point in a three-month period. This level of increased security would reflect a threat risk. There is still some circularity; investing in a market in increased security will cause it to happen. An investor willing to spend enough money on more security could overwhelm other investors and assure that security would be increased. DARPA hoped that investments would be of a low-enough dollar value that even individuals who recognized there was circularity would keep investing.

PAM markets could also have been based on contingent questions: "If A happens (US remains in Iraq more than two years), there is an X percent probability that B will happen (president of Syria will be overthrown by his own military high command)." One proposed market asked about the level of civil unrest in Saudi Arabia in the fourth quarter of 2004, conditional on the US withdrawing or not withdrawing its troops from the country by the end of the first quarter of that year.

Had the market been operational in 2003 during the debate on the Coalition's war with Iraq, a series of questions could have been posed about the three-month stability of the governments of Egypt, Syria, and Bahrain, either with an invasion or in the absence of one. Or a prediction market could have asked for expected world crude oil prices three months later, with or without an invasion.

The first PAM website offered ninety-five sample questions. Three of the more colorful examples related to an assassination of Palestinian leader Yasser Arafat by the first quarter of 2004, a North Korean missile attack on any other country by the fourth quarter of 2003, and the overthrow of King Hussein of Jordan by the fourth quarter of 2003. When DARPA reported on the progress of the project to Congress, it used as one example the question, "Will terrorists attack Israel with bio-weapons in the next year?" The hypothetical website question on assassination plus the biological war reference sealed PAM's fate.

When Senator Wyden and his colleague Byron Dorgan (D-North Dakota) learned of the examples, they went ballistic. They released an open letter in which they charged the Department of Defense with planning a "terror market" where individuals would be able to bet on "terrorist stocks." At a hastily called press conference on July 28, 2003, Wyden leaped off the "technology road map" bandwagon, leaving no doubt how far he had jumped. He called PAM "a federal betting parlor on atrocities and terrorism, it is ridiculous and it is grotesque." He asked, "What would happen if another country set up a betting parlor where people wagered on the assassination of an American political figure?"

That is a more interesting question than Senator Wyden may have realized at the time. Would a market on domestic political assassinations have any redeeming value? Would the Secret Service not want all possible information about the likelihood of an attempt on the life of whomever they were protecting? The higher the share price in such a market, the greater the perceived threat. The faster the market price increases, the more immediate the threat. The assassination target is alerted, and protective agencies get a heads-up.

DARPA was headed by the notorious retired Rear Admiral John M. Poindexter, who having earlier championed the prediction market idea, now distanced himself from it, and was thought to have urged his boss, Deputy Secretary of Defense Paul Wolfowitz, to do the same. Wolfowitz appeared before the Foreign Relations Committee the same day as the Wyden-Dorgan press conference. When asked about PAM, Wolfowitz claimed he had only learned about it from newspapers that morning. He said, "I share your shock at this kind of program. We'll find out about it, but it is being terminated." The next day the Pentagon canceled PAM. It was later revealed that the president's Council of Economic Advisors (CEA) were discussing a formal endorsement of PAM to head off cancellation, but the political decision to bail out came before the CEA could act.

Most editorials were critical of PAM, but focused on visceral and moral issues rather than anything analytical. There was little discussion of what PAM was intended to achieve. My favorite headline appeared in the *Santa Fe New Mexican*, "Dr. Strangelove Caught in Bizarre Betting Parlor." In one of the better discussions, the Indian newspaper *Business Line* pointed out that PAM was just a proposal for a free market, in the country that presented itself as the great proponent of free markets. *Business Line* noted that other payments offered for disreputable information raised few concerns. The Iraq Coalition had offered a $25 million bounty for the capture of Saddam and $15 million for each of his sons Uday and Qusay. Each was claimed and paid.

Congressman Wyden later suggested that his real concern was not PAM's objective, but rather that terrorists could engage in insider trading and profit from predicting incidents they would initiate. Or adversaries could trade to bias the outcome. This was possible, but unlikely. Any terrorist intending to blow up a refinery or hijack an oil supertanker would quickly figure out that he could do better by going long on oil futures or short-selling insurance company stock than by investing $100 in PAM.

There is another potential market-rigging problem that Wyden did not mention. Would terrorists try to mislead the Pentagon by investing against an outcome they knew would occur? Adam Meirowitz, a politics professor at Princeton, joked, "Sowing havoc among the infidels: PRICE-LESS." Or would a thousand other investors on the periphery of terrorist organizations, seeing that the market was badly mispriced, quickly bring it back in line with reality?

Another criticism of PAM was offered by Nobel economics laureate Joseph E. Stiglitz. He asked, "If this is such a good idea, why haven't the [commercial] markets created it?" The answer is that there is no incentive for a commercial organization to create a PAM-type prediction market with the hope of selling the data; there is no way to keep others from watching the market and obtaining the information for free.

A play-money market could offer PAM questions, but there would be little incentive for knowledgeable investors to take part. A real-money market like Intrade could create one, but there would be insufficient guarantee of anonymity for knowledgeable investors to risk taking part. This kind of market has to be run by an organization that will subsidize it and can be trusted to protect the identity of investors.

If terrorism questions on the website had not sunk PAM, it might have perished when members of Congress grasped its idea of extending internal intelligence agency markets to an external community. The logic of going external was straightforward; it was intended to attract foreigners with experience with Middle Eastern affairs, drawn by the possibility of making a profit and of proving themselves smarter than Americans.

These investors did not have to be in the intelligence field. Commercial aircraft crews who overnight once a week in Tehran might have a good sense of changing levels of hostility towards westerners. Syrian oil executives might be aware of exploration concessions being unexpectedly awarded to Chinese rather than American firms. Those contemplating regime change could also invest in markets. Yes, that includes assassins; that is how regime change takes place in a couple of the countries being examined.

An example of a market where external investors could have contributed involved the question of whether Iraq was, in 2001, importing specialized high-strength aluminum tubes in violation of western export restrictions. Many believed the tubes had legitimate industrial uses. US intelligence agencies argued the tubes' only use was in Iraq's reconstituted nuclear program. This argument became part of the United States' February 2003 weapons of mass destruction presentation at the United Nations. Future events proved the nuclear-use theory to be wrong. The tubes had been acquired in contravention of UN import restrictions, but for legitimate civilian uses. Analysts might have invested in this opinion had there been a market.

If PAM had survived, what other intelligence community issues might it have explored? In a pro–prediction market CIA briefing paper, analyst Puong Fei Yeh explored the balance of power in the Taiwan Strait and whether it had shifted against the United States and in favor of China. He suggested a market contract that read:

> In [a given three-month period], China will prevail against
> the United States in a clash in the Taiwan Strait, conditional
> on China successfully fielding supersonic sea-launched cruise
> missiles.

A high share price for this contract implies a high probability that investors think the balance of power in the Taiwan Straits would be in China's favor if there were a clash during the three-month period. The contingency provision indicates that fielding supersonic naval cruise missiles is a critical factor in China's success, and implies that the US Navy does not have adequate countermeasures to such missiles. The cruise missile contingency could be tested with a second contract:

> Given China's current rate of research and development, China will successfully field-test a supersonic sea-launched cruise missile [in the next six months].

A third question could be used to test the premise of a clash in the Taiwan Strait:

> China's leaders will seek to forcibly reunite Taiwan with the mainland during [a given year], conditional on Taiwan introducing a referendum on independence.

Yeh's proposals illustrate a key requirement of every prediction market: the need for an explicit and narrowly focused question. No one would have had the foresight in 2001 to propose:

> Al-Qaeda will hijack a commercial aircraft in the next [six months] and fly it into the World Trade Center.

But proposing a series of contracts, with the first being:

> Al-Qaeda will mount a terrorist attack against the United States in 2001.

and including:

> Terrorists will hijack a commercial aircraft and use it as a flying bomb in 2001.

would have presented more narrowly focused outcomes.

In 2001, there was good reason to ask such questions. Not only had the FBI received tips, but the US National Security Agency (NSA) in Fort Meade, Maryland, had communication intercepts indicating that a major Al-Qaeda operation would be mounted against US interests in the second half of 2001. The idea of using an airliner as a suicide bomb had been discussed in military literature as early as 1978, and was a central plot feature in the best-selling 1996 Tom Clancy novel *Clear and Present Danger*.

Markets might have also been used to predict Coalition success in calming the Iraq insurgency. A series of contracts could have been offered to measure civil stability and economic progress in the country:

> Insurgent bomb attacks in Baghdad will decrease from the 2007 level by at least 50 percent in 2008 [they did].

and

> Oil output from the non-Kurdish areas of Iraq will rise from 575,000 barrels a day in 2007 to at least 900,000 barrels a day in 2008 [it did].

These questions could have been posed as six-month, one-year, and two-year contracts by changing percentage increases compared with the previous period. If analysts believed the Coalition was losing its fight with insurgents in the short run but President Bush's "Surge" would be successful in the medium term, the share price for a short-term contract would be lower than that of a longer-term contract. If analysts thought insurgents would adapt to the Surge, the share price for a short-term contract on these questions would be higher than that for a longer-term contract. The share price for a contract at different points in time would give politicians and military commanders a real-time evaluation of perceived progress, or lack of it.

Intrade could have run markets on the probability of an American or Israeli air strike on Iran. Who would know of a pending air strike? Several thousand people might. Most would be military and unwilling to risk a court martial or worse for leaking information. But the several thousand each have friends and relatives. There are civilian employees at air bases, plus many people in the vicinity who would take note of the deployment of in-flight refueling aircraft, or increased activity on bases, or call-ups of air force reservists.

The friends and relatives might not recognize the circularity involved with an air-strike market. *Circularity* here means that if a strike seemed imminent, information leaks would drive up the contract price, providing Iranians both warning and motivation to moderate their position.

Diplomats from other countries would have the opportunity to mediate. Tracking the price of this contract during mediation would enable both sides to better understand the impact of their statements and actions. The action of many traders investing in an air strike makes it less likely to happen.

Other terrorism-related contracts come to mind. Consider their application to the two most serious American foreign policy blunders in the last few years. First was the failure by Donald Rumsfeld, Paul Wolfowitz, and others to look past al-Qaeda and Osama bin Laden and understand the long-term threat posed by the Taliban. The second was the failure to anticipate the emergence of the Waziristan area of northwest Pakistan as a haven for Islamic extremists. Both seem, in retrospect, to have been recognized by many experts on central Asia. With properly worded questions, PAM might have highlighted the issues early.

There was another market option considered but not used. This was a DARPA-run prediction market internal to US intelligence agencies, plus a commercial market open to all. The two would ask exactly the same questions at the same time. The two markets would end up with the same security prices and predictions, because any decent intelligence agency programmer could write a hedging bot that would buy or sell in each market until prices were equalized, just as happens in election markets.

A first cousin to PAM is Intellipedia, three wikis now in use by American intelligence agencies (a wiki is a collaborative website whose content can be edited by anyone who has access to it). Intellipedia uses *Wikipedia* software and collects anonymous information on intelligence topics. It has the same goal as prediction markets: to get better answers by inducing people to disclose what they know. In the first year of operation, there were thirty thousand pages of content from about twelve hundred contributors. Intellipedia is classified and accessible only by the intelligence community. It does not provide the same incentive to contribute or the same structured questions as would a prediction market. It does have the advantage of not attracting congressional bombast.

Prediction market contracts like those proposed for PAM are now run privately. At least three Washington companies provide confidential market data to US intelligence agencies. Some analysts are former DARPA employees. It is not clear whether the markets operate only internally in intelligence agencies or whether they are open to a select group of external investors.

Do these markets offer markets on assassination or terrorism? During the last year of the George W. Bush administration, government officials largely ignored the taunts and threats of Venezuelan president Hugo Chávez and his actions to drive Conoco and Exxon from the country. It was widely believed in Washington that one reason for this benign neglect was a prediction market conclusion that Chávez was at high risk of assassination by his own military. If true, it was one of those markets when a high probability did not translate into an event.

When the PAM project was ridiculed and killed, DARPA analysts had their revenge. Someone whispered to commercial prediction site TradeSports.com that a fun market could be launched on whether their project's suddenly unsupportive boss, John Poindexter, would still hold his job in three months.

The market opened on July 29, 2003, with a 40 percent probability that Poindexter would be gone three months later. Two days later the price rose to 80 percent. Rumors of his resignation surfaced that afternoon. Whether the rumors caused the run up in the market or the market produced the rumors is unknown. No resignation came that day. The market slipped a bit until August 12, when it jumped to 96 percent. Poindexter released his letter of resignation late that afternoon.

A US government intelligence agency tool intended to monitor terrorist communications is being used as a form of involuntary prediction market, similar to but vastly larger in scale than Google Trends. As part of President Bush's Terrorist Surveillance Program, the NSA began at the time of the 9/11 attacks to collect and analyze information from the nation's major telecommunication companies. A presidential order authorized the NSA to monitor US phone conversations, e-mail, Web browsing, and corporate private network traffic.

The NSA is part of the Department of Defense; it circumvented the prohibition against involvement on US soil by partnering with the Department of Homeland Security on the program. In July 2008, Congress gave retroactive immunity to anyone who had taken part in the program, and to companies like AT&T that had cooperated. At the end of 2010, the NSA database was estimated to contain 4.1 trillion call records.

The intention was to use sophisticated algorithms to search for keywords thought to be associated with terrorist communication. In 2007, this mandate was expanded to analyzing the frequency of keywords associated with the emotional state of the country. The words used by each correspondent suggest their future activities, concerns, and state of mind. The NSA project, code-named *Stellar Wind*, became a plot component in Dan Brown's 2009 best-seller, *The Lost Symbol*. In the book, it is described as a way of "taking the nation's temperature," of measuring its emotional state. Brown's character Trish Dunne describes, "In the event, for example, of a terrorist attack, the government could use data fields to measure the shift in America's psyche and better advise the president of the emotional impact of the event." The UK's security service M16 operates a parallel system called Echelon.

After the financial meltdown of 2008, the NSA is reported to have begun mining the communications database for indicators of confidence in the US financial system. This NSA involuntary market considers 3.5 billion new predictions each day. If it can be expanded to monitor Internet telephone calls (Voice over Internet Protocol, or VoIP), such as Skype, that number goes to 4 billion.

It is hard to know how many terrorists Stellar Wind might detect, because the keyword and emotional indicator phrases work best with native English speakers communicating in English. It also works best with terrorists not savvy enough to communicate through simple code phrases, "Uncle Harry arrives Tuesday at three p.m." But the system might work for other monitoring tasks. All that is required is selection of the right keywords and indicators.

I am curious about how many NSA analysts, hunting for terrorist communication, may have intercepted early drafts of this book, given that its working title was *The Saddam Market* (there was in early drafts a chapter describing a successful prediction market run on the timing of Saddam

Hussein's capture). Many individual chapters were sent by Internet for comment by others, with "Saddam Market" in the subject line.

If markets can be used to predict how long John Poindexter will keep his job, could they be used on more serious matters of government policy? The answer is yes; the next chapter provides examples.

13

Government Markets

Decision markets will one day revolutionize governance, both public and private.

—Robin Hanson, professor, George Mason University

BAD GOVERNMENT DECISIONS at all levels are frequently blamed on some form of information failure. Either there is too little information about the consequences of the alternatives being considered, or decision makers are limited to information provided by staff researchers or lobbying groups. While it would never replace the deliberative process in a democracy, there are ways that markets might be used at every level of government to mitigate these problems. Where the market signaled an outcome dramatically different from that expected by staff people, the subject might be revisited.

At the local government level, a promising use of markets comes in predicting crime rates and figuring out how to reduce them. Economists M. Todd Henderson, Justin Wolfers, and Eric Zitzewitz have suggested some fascinating possibilities. At present, predicting how much crime might occur in an area utilizes the experience and gut feeling of senior police officers, or uses quant analysis based on maps overlaid with locations of recent crimes. These are backward-looking techniques, subject to a lot of biases by the individuals involved. The methods work reasonably well for car theft and petty larceny. They do not work well for burglary, assault, and murder.

A simple market might ask whether the rate of reported burglaries in the Prospect Heights section of Brooklyn, New York, will be higher over the next three months than during the same period the year before. Police officials, academics, criminologists, and the general public—including current and potential criminals—could invest in the market. The market price aggregates the information available from each trader. Anyone with reason to believe that the burglary rate would be lower this year (the strategist of the Prospect Heights burglary gang has retired to Miami) would sell short the contract, expecting to profit as criminologists and budget-motivated police officials invested in a higher burglary rate.

To my knowledge, no crime prediction market has yet been run, but everything we know about prediction markets suggests it would work. There are currently a lot of obstacles that prevent information about criminal activity reaching the police. Those with the most valuable information about crime—cops on foot patrol, citizens who observe their neighbors' activities or overhear conversations at a bar, and criminals themselves—will not necessarily report to the authorities. The potential costs in terms of time and risk are high, and the personal benefits are low. Markets provide a financial incentive to disclose. Equally important, markets offer anonymity.

Investors also don't have to puzzle over whom to contact with information. If you live in Prospect Heights and overhear a plan to hijack cargo from a recently docked ship, whom do you call? The local police precinct? The New York State Police? The FBI? The Bureau of Alcohol, Tobacco, Firearms and Explosives? The Coast Guard? Your local borough politician? Private security guards on the dock? How do you keep your information from being dismissed as fake or self-serving, or as coming from someone mentally unbalanced, particularly if you have no intention of identifying yourself or the people you were eavesdropping on? The easiest solution is to say nothing.

Predicting crime rates has some things in common with predicting terrorism. What is being predicted is a combination of the underlying crime rate and expected police response. Police may respond to a prediction of more crime in an area by assigning more officers. But the police response is not expected to be so substantial as to invalidate the prediction. Investors would likely ignore the link between predicting crime and more policing, as they ignore the link between predicting terrorism and increased antiterrorist activities.

There is also the underlying problem that markets do not just aggregate information, they broadcast it to anyone who checks the market price. Burglars could monitor what areas have high predicted break-in rates and then shift their activity to districts with lower predicted rates and less police presence. However, this may be giving too much credit to criminal planners.

Public policy toward crime could also be investigated through prediction markets. Think of a market that asked the incidence of street robbery in a section of Brooklyn, and a second market that asked the incidence conditional on ten extra officers being assigned to the area. Other contracts could be based on the crime rate, conditional on longer minimum jail terms in sentencing guidelines, on antigang efforts, or on availability of government-funded entry-level jobs in the area.

Should criminals, those currently in jail or on parole, be allowed to take part and profit from these markets? This is politically sensitive in the same way as allowing terrorists to trade is. But criminals have a lot of information about future crime patterns. Providing an incentive to reveal this information is not that different, in principle, from offering reduced prison sentences for those who testify against their partners in crime.

Could a market approach be used at the state government level to set highway speed limits by allowing motorists to predict safe speeds under current conditions? The existing system—one posted speed for all conditions, day and night—is not very satisfactory. Around Toronto, the speed limit on four- and six-lane highways is 100 km (about 63 miles) per hour. This is lower than it was on two-lane highways in the 1950s, in spite of today's better-engineered roads and the superior steering, tires, and braking systems of twenty-first-century cars. Politicians don't raise speed limits because they don't want to risk being blamed for fatal accidents. Rather, they expect police to be lenient in enforcement.

Police generally do give motorists what is called a "20 km over" (about 13 mph) on major highways, to a point where anyone traveling at the posted speed limit is at risk of being rear-ended by an eighteen-wheeler. Police then periodically crack down with a ticketing blitz, often in response to political pressure to generate more revenue. Speeders are caught easily; they have been lulled by the period of 20-over. Ticketed motorists incur higher insurance premiums and dislike traffic cops. The police in turn dislike the political pressure to produce revenue.

Simply resetting limits to 120 km (73 mph) with strict enforcement offers problems. While this speed is appropriate under most conditions, there are periods of rain, fog, or ice when even 100 km is dangerous. Most drivers do choose a safe speed for the conditions they face; they have a lot to lose in the event of an accident.

What would happen if roadside radar, positioned every 10 km (6.2 miles) on major highways, monitored the average or median speed of passing vehicles, and posted the number on overhead illuminated signs as the current speed limit? There could be upper and lower permissible limits, say 120 km (73 mph) and 80 km (49 mph). This uses the aggregated wisdom of motorists about what is safe. This market approach might actually make the policing job easier.

The police would need a record of posted speed in each segment of the highway, but would then be working with a realistic speed limit, which could be strictly enforced. Motorists' collective prediction of a safe speed would be seen by all as a more logical process than a random "gift" of kilometers-over by whatever police officer draws the short straw for traffic duty on a particular stretch of highway.

Let's look at a less controversial state government example—a department of prisons' proposal to open a high-security prison in a location far from any urban center. Department staff prepare a briefing paper on the pros and cons of the new location. Department officials can check their conclusions by running markets to predict unemployment rates, housing values, and prisoner recidivism rates with and without the prison being located in the rural location under consideration. Recidivism is relevant, because a rural location makes it harder for family members to visit inmates and maintain family bonds.

How about a market to signal the state's position on who should marry? My literary agent John Pearce, having just come from one of those weddings where guests mumble, "Look who she's marrying; it will never last," suggests a very contemporary use for a prediction market—as a replacement for the moment in a civil wedding ceremony where the officiant says, "If any man can show just cause why these two should not be lawfully joined together, speak now or forever hold your peace." It is a time of high drama; will an ex-lover appear, proclaiming his love, as Dustin Hoffman's character famously did in the 1967 movie *The Graduate*? Will a not-quite-divorced spouse materialize?

John suggests this part of the ceremony be replaced by a designated individual rising at that point to announce the results of a prediction market run for family and friends prior to the service. The market will ask whether the couple is expected to be together five years after the ceremony. If the revealed probability is less than 80 percent, the officiant would perform a commitment ceremony rather than a government-sanctioned marriage. If they were still together five years later, the couple could hold a recommitment ceremony, and if they scored 80 percent on that occasion could become legally married. And no, John is not serious, but the idea does make you think of what other creative uses there might be for government markets.

At the federal level, would a prediction market be able to provide insight into one of the most difficult problems in health-care policy, the merits of a government-run prescription drug program? Assume President Obama proposed (as he several times suggested during his 2008 campaign) that as part of health-care reform legislation, the Department of Health pay for and oversee distribution of all prescription drugs in the United States. This would make life-prolonging drugs universally available. It would also require drug price controls, because there would no longer be any resistance from patients or insurers to price increases. The incidence and severity of disease would drop, but lower profit margins would reduce each drug company's incentive to spend the millions of dollars required to bring each new medication to market.

How does a policy maker measure this trade-off? It is difficult to find an expert who does not carry a conflict of interest. Public health agency doctors and many other physicians support the Obama option; drug company employees and many university researchers favor the status quo. A prediction market might produce a less biased estimate; experts on both sides could offer anonymous views. Using a prediction market would also allow policymakers to take ideology and politics—and their own biases—out of the decision process.

Could a federal government agency use a market to predict and avert emergencies? A 2008 horror story involving Atomic Energy of Canada (AECL) suggests they should try. AECL is a government-owned corporation that operates a nuclear reactor in Chalk River, Ontario. When the reactor is operational, it produces more than half of the world's radioisotopes. These are used in medical imaging and diagnostic scans for a long list of medical problems, including cancer, heart disease, and fractures. There are no ready substitutes for isotopes; they have a half-life measured in days, and cannot be stockpiled.

The fifty-year-old Chalk River nuclear facility was built on an earthquake fault line. The area has not had a major quake in the last century, but there have been a number of minor ones—in the 3.0–3.6 magnitude range—most recently in January 2008. The quakes are strong enough to shake things up, but so far, not strong enough to knock anything down.

On November 18, 2007, the reactor was shut down for maintenance. Inspectors found that a mandatory safety upgrade that involved connecting cooling pumps to an emergency power supply had never been carried out. The pumps are needed to prevent an accident in case of a loss of regular power, which might occur with an earthquake. Inspectors refused to allow the reactor to be started up again, triggering a worldwide shortage of isotopes. The Canadian Parliament had to vote to overrule the regulator and order the reactor restarted.

Senior AECL managers claimed they had not understood the necessity of having pumps connected to the emergency power supply. An investigator from Washington, DC–based consultant Talisman International reported that many people knew the pumps were not connected. Some would have known the safety concern, but felt no obligation to alert senior management or anyone else. One of my former graduate students, a nuclear engineer, says this "see no evil, hear no evil" is standard operating procedure in the nuclear industry, especially for young engineers communicating with superiors. The shutdown seems to represent a classic case where no one wants to pass bad news up the hierarchy, and there are no other mechanisms in place to disclose it.

The AECL problem is reminiscent of the findings of the Columbia Accident Investigation Board (CAIB), which attributed the *Columbia* space shuttle disaster to NASA's failure to use information already available within the agency and the supplier community. The CAIB said the hierarchical structure of NASA meant knowledge widely held by low-level engineers would not percolate up through the agency's hierarchy.

How could a predictions market have alleviated the AECL problem? A routine question about the duration of a planned maintenance shutdown would have suggested hidden problems. Another question about the ability to meet demand for isotopes over a three- or six-month period would have produced a warning. Plant engineers, marketing staff, corporate partners, and the isotope-using community could invest in the market.

Did AECL learn from this incident and rectify problems in its communication process? Well, no. Eighteen months later, on May 15, 2009, the reactor had to be shut down again after a heavy-water leak was detected within the facility. Officials first said it would be out of service for a month so that repair options for the corroded tubes could be considered. Employees then pointed out a number of other corrosion problems, and the shutdown period was extended to "six months to a year."

Another federal government example is provided by Tom W. Bell at Chapman Law School in Los Angeles. The Defense Department has an ongoing concern: how to predict cost overruns on weapon procurement programs, and whether an overrun will be so large as to trigger a breach under the Nunn-McCurdy Amendment to the 1982 Defense Procurement Act. Such a breach would endanger the program and under some circumstances, would lead to its cancellation.

Bell suggests that the Department of Defense create a prediction market for the claim, "Over the next six months, the VXXX Helicopter Program [as an example] will trigger a Nunn-McCurdy breach." Employees of contractors or subcontractors or others with firsthand knowledge could trade on the claim (or Bell suggests, be required to trade). A high probability of a breach would alert program managers and executive branch agencies to the possible problem more quickly than current monitoring methods.

Could markets be used to predict a federal Supreme Court decision before a case is heard? If it could, and such a prediction was seen to be reliable, a market could save litigants a great deal of time and millions of dollars in legal costs.

The first indicator that this might work comes from the performance of law school students. As pointed out in a study by Miriam Cherry at University of the Pacific and Robert Rogers of the *Legal Times*, most law school final exams include at least one "issue spotter" question. This requires students to read the facts of a hypothetical court case, extract the legal issues, and analyze them based on the legal precedents covered in the course. The key is the student's ability to spot the salient issues. Almost no student spots every relevant issue in the case. When student exams are aggregated, they do cover all the issues. Often the class spots issues that go beyond the ones the professor intended to include. The consensus of the class almost always reaches the correct legal decision. The law school class in aggregate is much smarter than the student who achieves the best grade in the exam question, and sometimes smarter than the professor.

In November 2009, a market was set up by Josh Blackman at Penn State University's Dickinson School of Law. Called Fantasy SCOTUS, it asks players to predict whether the Supreme Court will affirm or reverse a lower court, what the split will be (5-4, 7-2), and how individual justices will vote. The top players are appellate court clerks (Supreme Court clerks are not allowed to take part). Blackman says the results are better than any other source he knows that predicts Court decisions.

In comparison to some other examples in previous chapters, this is a simple prediction problem. Investors need only evaluate how nine justices will vote, rather than, for example, how millions of people will evaluate a forthcoming movie. The prior voting records and ideological and religious preferences of the nine are known. Further, the decision is bounded. There are only two options to choose from: affirm the lower court decision or reverse it. (A market could not easily be used to predict the outcome of jury trials in lower courts. Nothing is known of jury members, their ideologies or other biases, or what instructions the judge will give them. There is no previous juror record to rely on.)

Who might be invited to invest in a real SCOTUS market? Include anyone who has argued a case before the Supreme Court, academics who study the court, and those who have clerked at the court in the past. The necessary diversity comes with the differing backgrounds and political leanings within this group.

As Cherry and Rogers point out, professional recognition from successful prediction may be reward enough to make this market function. Whoever makes the most accurate predictions over time will come to be known as the Warren Buffett of Supreme Court prognostication.

Economist Robin Hanson has suggested a system of government based on markets, which he calls *futarchy*. Here, elected representatives decide what issues should be part of national policy, then national prediction markets determine how to achieve those goals. The democratic process specifies what we want, and prediction markets suggest how to get it. Hanson proposes that the prediction market result be binding on legislators, rather than advisory.

Futarchy may seem reminiscent of the famous California state system where voters can initiate a referendum question. If the referendum passes, the state constitution is then amended, usually to lock in spending or to impose limitations on the taxing process. Result: at the time of writing, in mid-2011, the State of California had so much referendum-mandated spending and such constrained taxing powers that it was, by any definition, bankrupt. Its bond rating was A–, lowest of the fifty states and barely higher than junk (or Greece).

However, in the California referendum system, corporations or other interest groups sponsor most initiatives, send hundreds of independent contractors out to do the collection, and pay a fixed amount per name collected. Then the sponsor advertises to promote one side of the initiative. It is hardly a "no-outside-influence" market, nor an example of futarchy.

Hanson's logic is intriguing. He asks, in an article of the same name, "Shall We Vote on Values but Bet on Beliefs?" Most government decisions involve a combination of facts and values. Does global warming exist, and if so, what should elected officials do about it? The first of these is about facts, the second about values. What would be the effect on investment in new technologies if the capital gains tax were cut in half? "What will happen to investment?" is the factual part, and whether the tax should be reduced is a question of values. The futarchy system could be used for policy issues as diverse as gun control and extended US involvement in Afghanistan. The idea got so much attention that the term futarchy was named by the *New York Times* as one of the buzzwords of 2008.

14

Long-Term Markets

*I expect there will be some failures . . . I don't anticipate any
serious problems of that sort among the large internationally
active banks.*

—Ben Bernanke, Federal Reserve Chairman, February 28, 2008

*Professor Goddard does not know the relation between action and
reaction and the need to have something better than a vacuum
against which to react. He seems to lack the basic knowledge ladled
out daily in high schools.*

—A 1921 *New York Times* editorial about Robert Goddard's work
on rocket propulsion, nominated as the worst *Times* editorial
of all time. The newspaper published a correction on June 17,
1969, motivated by the *Apollo* crew beginning their journey to
the moon.

IT IS CONVENTIONAL FINANCIAL wisdom that over a period of time, a
broad index such as the S&P 500 will outperform almost any combination of investment funds. Warren Buffett, the CEO of investment fund
Berkshire Hathaway and the man some believe to be the world's smartest
investor, agrees. He thinks the wisdom of individual investors whose collective decisions determine the level of the S&P 500 will outperform any
group of experts.

On January 1, 2008, Buffett wagered $1 million on this belief. Accepting the bet was Ted Seides of Protégé Partners LLC, a New York City money management firm that runs hedge funds. Buffett's bet was that over a ten-year period, the Vanguard 500 Index Investor Fund, a low-fee fund that tracks the S&P 500 index, would beat the average net return of any five hedge funds picked by Seides. The five were not publicly divulged, although Protégé is certainly one. Each of the five is itself a mutual fund of funds, so the comparison is with a cross-section of funds chosen as the best. The bet is between Buffett (not Berkshire Hathaway) and Protégé (the company, not the five funds).

Each side put up $320,000. The $640,000 total was used to purchase a zero-coupon US Treasury bond to be redeemed, with accumulated interest, for $1 million at the conclusion of the bet in 2018. If Protégé wins, the money goes to the London charity Friends of Absolute Return for Kids. If Buffett wins, it goes to Girls Incorporated of Omaha.

Because we don't know which funds are involved, we don't know their ten-year performance. If you compare the Protégé fund to the S&P 500 Index, the results are mixed. From the five and a half years between its start-up to the placing of the bet, the Protégé fund was up 95 percent after fees. The Vanguard fund gained 64 percent over the same period. In that comparison, Protégé wins. If you add one more year to the beginning of January 2009, or three years to January 2011, thus incorporating the 2008 market meltdown, Vanguard wins.

The structure of the bet is a compromise. Buffett initially proposed that ten funds be included, which would have improved his chances a lot. That proposal would have allowed one hundred fund-years to mess up (ten years times ten funds) rather than fifty (ten times five).

Buffett insisted on the ten-year period. Using a shorter period would be making the same mistake individuals make when choosing among mutual funds, basing a decision on one, three, or five years of prior results. That is like evaluating basketball superstar LeBron James on his uninspired performance for the Miami Heat over the five games of the 2011 NBA final. When it comes to investment performance, longer time periods are more indicative of skill.

Protégé responded with a proposal that only three of the five funds had to beat the S&P 500 over a ten-year period. That concession would have improved Protégé's chances; it would be like judging LeBron's performance only against teams with losing records.

Central to Buffett's argument as to why he will win is the high fee structure charged by investment managers. A fund of funds normally charges a 1 percent annual management fee plus 5 percent of the capital gains. The underlying funds charge their own management fee, typically 1.5 percent, plus 20 percent of any gains they achieve. The Vanguard Fund charges large investors only 0.7 percent.

The first three years after the bet showed mixed results. During financially tumultuous 2008, Protégé fell 24 percent and Buffet's index fund lost 37 percent. In 2009, Protégé gained 16 percent and the index fund 27 percent. In 2010 it was Protégé up 9 percent, the index fund up 15 percent. Over the three-year period, Protégé led with a 4.2 percent overall loss versus the index fund's 8 percent overall loss.

Buffett has said he calculates his chance of being ahead at the end of ten years at 60 percent. Protégé calculates its chances at 85 percent. The San Francisco foundation Long Bets, which administers the wager, has run its own market on the outcome. Consistently from the first day the bet was posted, just under 80 percent of those offering predictions thought Buffett would win.

There is another reason why, over a ten-year period, an index such as the S&P 500 should outperform an investment fund. Investment seems like an activity that combines skill and luck. With the collective investment decisions that make up the S&P 500, good luck and bad luck would then average out, and the wisdom of collective investors would prevail.

At this point, the reader will suddenly have raised at least one eyebrow: is stock picking not a skill activity like chess playing, rather than one of pure chance like playing a slot machine? Or is it, like poker, a mix of skill and chance? A test of the degree to which an activity involves luck or skill is whether you can lose on purpose. Playing chess, it is easy to intentionally lose. With a slot machine it is impossible. Is stock picking more like chess or slots?

In 2008, John Rogers, founder of Chicago money manager investment company Ariel Investments, asked seventy-one of his colleagues to each pick ten stocks that would underperform the market in the second quarter. Only nineteen of them succeeded; fifty-two tried to lose, and failed. The average return on the intentionally losing portfolios was 30 percent, double the return of the S&P 500 over the same period. At least in the short run, good stock picking seems to contain a high component of luck.

Long Bets, which is managing the Buffett-Protégé stake, is part of the nonprofit Long Now Foundation, and an example of how markets can be used to gain insight into longer-term trends. The Foundation was started in April 2002 by *Wired* editor Kevin Kelly and Stewart Brand of *The Whole Earth Catalogue.* Funding came from Jeff Bezos, founder and CEO of Amazon.com. The goal was to raise the quality of long-term prediction. The idea is straightforward: offer a controversial prediction, post your arguments, and back your conviction with cash. The Foundation adjudicates the result. The website, www.longnow.org, has become a futurist blog site.

Long Bets focuses on predictions of societal or scientific importance. It asks participants to state the logic behind their betting position. Whether the prediction turns out to be right or wrong, it is fascinating to follow the thought process, to capture the rationale of each investor.

The site charges $50 to publish a prediction. If someone wants to challenge, it becomes a wager. The minimum wager is $1,000, with the money placed in a Long Bets investment account. The minimum was set high to discourage the uncertain investor and to allow Long Bets to focus on well-argued issues. The minimum term of a prediction is two years; most are five years or more. Odds are always even, the result is always win/lose.

In 2002, the Foundation added a "voting on bets" feature. This is an ego investment (no money) for those voting on the outcome; each predictor has to self-identify and state the logic behind his or her choice. Long Bets hopes a lot of thought will go into the justification. Individuals can only vote once and can't change their vote, so the long-term prediction aspect involves tracking the vote percentage over each three-month period.

When bet terms are met, either because a predicted event happens or the period expires, the money is paid to the charity named by the winner. Because the bettor does not get to keep winnings, there is no suggestion of illegal gambling. Half the interest goes to cover Long Bet's administrative costs.

In another widely publicized Long Bets wager, Microsoft's chief technical officer Craig Mundie bet Google's Eric Schmidt $2,000 that "commercial airline passengers will routinely fly in pilotless planes by 2030." Schmidt does not suggest this is technically difficult. Aircraft already take off, fly long distances, and land under computer control; military drones do it hundreds of times each day. Schmidt, himself a pilot, thinks there will still have to be one on board to reassure passengers that someone is available in case of an unpredictable event. Schmidt offers an industry joke about passengers being less than happy when they settle in their seats and hear a monotone recording, "This is your pilot speaking, speaking, speaking."

Mundie, in turn, thinks that passengers will trust technology to such a degree that they will want to remove any risk of a human second-guessing the computer. What Long Bets is running is a prediction exercise on future public acceptance of high technology. It is a comfort test—not, "Is technology safe?" but, "Does the public believe that technology is safe?"

In 2010, Mundie's no-pilot bet had 28 percent support, and Schmidt's need-pilot had 71 percent. Schmidt's need-pilot rose—and stayed up—after the January 2009 incident in which US Airways flight 1549 collided with a formation of geese on takeoff from LaGuardia airport in New York, lost all engine power, but was landed safely in the Hudson River by pilot Sully Sullenberger.

Wagers that play out over a period of time, like all prediction markets, have to be carefully worded and qualified. A Long Bet between Dave Winer, a prolific blogger and CEO of UserLand.com, and Martin Nisenholtz, CEO of *New York Times Digital*, read, "In a Google search of five keywords or phrases representing the top five news stories of 2007, [web logs] will rank higher than the *New York Times* website." The premise of the bet was that readers would come to trust noncommercial blogs on the Internet over news stories from perhaps the most highly respected commercial print media.

When the question came up for adjudication in 2007, one issue was which list of top 2007 stories to use. Long Bets chose the Associated Press list over several other candidates, because the AP list existed in 2002. The top five stories were, in reverse order, Chinese exports, oil prices, the Iraq War, the mortgage crisis, and the Virginia Tech mass murder.

The next question was, "What is a web log?" Does *Wikipedia* qualify? Do you include the *Times* blog and other commercial blogs, or just noncommercial websites? Long Bets decided to count anything that would have been recognized as a blog in 2002, excluding both the NYT site and *Wikipedia*.

If you added up Google page-rank standings, blogs won, 4:1. If you averaged page ranks of the NYT versus blogs, blogs won big. If you averaged the rank of user-submitted content versus commercial content, commercial news outlets won. Long Bets decided that, two out of three, Dave Winer and blogs won the wager.

The real winner in the five years following the bet was *Wikipedia*, founded a few months before the 2002 bet. *Wikipedia* in 2007 ranked higher on four of the five stories—all but Chinese exports.

Another Long Bet involves whether computers will successfully impersonate a human; specifically, whether a computer will pass the Turing test by 2029. In 1950, mathematician Alan Turing proposed a way to determine whether a machine had achieved human-level intelligence. In his test (and in the Long Bet wager), a panel of three judges interview both the machine and a human, each through a text-based messaging system. The judges ask questions about personal and social relationships, and about arts and science. They try to determine which respondent is the carbon-based life form. A computer program that fools the judges, or at least produces uncertainty, passes the Turing test.

The idea that a computer might pass such a test resurfaced in 2005 with the publication of Ray Kurzweil's *The Singularity Is Near: When Humans Transcend Biology*. Kurzweil argues that increasing computer power will result in machine dominance. Kurzweil has bet $10,000 that a computer will win the Turing challenge. He argues that in thirty years we will have a computer that can learn—a more articulate version of HAL 9000 from *2001: A Space Odyssey*, claiming, "It's only a matter of software development and modeling the computer after the human brain."

Mitch Kapor, founder of Lotus software, disagrees. Kapor says that without human experience a computer cannot answer questions about quintessentially human matters. He says that the whole brain-as-computer idea "is only a metaphor, much like viewing the heart as a pump. We're undervaluing and under-appreciating ourselves if we think a computer is going to pass us." This Turing test wager is, of course, not really about computer development, but rather about future roles of humans and machines in society. In 2010 Kurzweil's "computer will win" had 56 percent support on Long Bets, and Kapor's "computer won't exceed us" had 44 percent.

Human-level machine intelligence has already been demonstrated in narrowly defined areas. Garry Kasparov said, after the famous 1997 exhibition match in which he was defeated by IBM's Deep Blue, that he "saw deep intelligence and creativity in the machine's moves," and playing ability indistinguishable from that of a human chess master.

You have almost certainly taken (and passed) a reverse Turing test, to prove you are not a computer. When you make an online purchase or post a blog, you are asked to examine a line of distorted text, then to type the letters into a box. This is to prevent spammers from writing software that emulates humans in order to steal passwords or buy all the prime tickets on Ticketmaster. Humans are much better at reading these characters than is pattern-recognition software.

The online puzzles are called CAPTCHAs, a term coined by professor Luis von Ahn at Carnegie Mellon University. The acronym stands for Completely Automated Public Turing Test to Tell Computers and Humans

Apart. Completing a CAPTCHA shows there is a human at the other end of the transaction. But it is a fleeting success. The CAPTCHA system has to be reworked every six months, as machine vision catches up. Computer programs are expected to equal humans in solving CAPTCHAs by 2014.

Other Long Bets wager challenges cover some exotic topics. Theoretical physicist Freeman Dyson offers the following: "The first discovery of extraterrestrial life will be someplace other than on a planet or on a satellite of a planet." Dyson's explanation is that if extraterrestrial life exists, it might have adapted to living in a vacuum. If so, it must have lenses or mirrors to focus sunlight and keep warm. These will reflect sunlight in a narrow beam back toward the sun. If a telescope sees a bright reflection, it means life. It is like seeing the eyes of an animal caught in headlights. As of 2010, only 29 percent of Long Bets comments favored Dyson's view.

Some very smart people offer wagers on the Long Bets site; Warren Buffett, Craig Mundie, and Eric Schmidt have been mentioned. The list also includes Nathan Myhrvold, former chief technology officer of Microsoft; Gordon Bell, senior researcher at Microsoft; and Jim Griffin of Cherry Lane Digital. Where else can you suggest an issue of importance to your business or to society and, for $1,000, have some of the brightest minds in the world offer insights and predict the outcome?

One prediction that was not accepted by Long Bets quickly migrated to a commercial market. Wharton business school professor Scott Armstrong concluded that if you had to forecast what the average temperature would be in ten years, "the same as today" would be more accurate than the Intergovernmental Panel on Climate Change forecast of a rise of three-tenths of a degree Celsius, the figure cited by Nobel laureate and former US Vice President Al Gore.

Armstrong offered to bet Gore $20,000 that the naive, no-change forecast would prove more accurate than Gore's IPCC figure. The winner was to be decided at the meeting of the International Symposium of Forecasting in 2018. The money would have been placed in trust and given to a charity chosen by the winner. Gore responded that he does not make financial bets.

Intrade then set up a prediction market for the proposition, "Gore vs. Armstrong," but over a three-year time period rather than ten. The Armstrong price remained around $62. Taking the Gore side would cost $38 to win $100. Given the overwhelming scientific consensus that Gore claims in talking about global warming, this would seem a pretty good investment. It turns out that any ten-year forecast of "no change" during the past 150 years would have won 68 percent of the time, despite the fact that, long-term, temperature is trending up. A three-year forecast of no change should carry a very high probability of being true.

The benefit from using some form of market for long-term predictions is clear. Think of the everyday business terms that might follow the phrase *long-term*—market trends, capital markets, economic cycles, health care trends, housing starts, Chinese market development, and private-label market share. All that is required to harvest the benefit is creativity and some out-of-the-box thinking.

PART FOUR

Making
Markets Work

15

When No One Wants to Know

The most mystifying thing about [prediction] markets is how little interest corporate America has shown in them . . . companies have remained, for the most part, indifferent to this source of potentially excellent information.

—James Surowiecki, *The Wisdom of Crowds*

In theory there is no difference between theory and practice. In practice there is.

—Yogi Berra, baseball manager and philosopher

EACH TIME I GIVE a talk on the wonders of prediction markets, the first raised hand comes attached to a question as to why so many companies are still uncomfortable with the concept. Why is there indifference to such a potentially great source of information? After all, executives accept the idea of shareholders trading on a stock exchange to aggregate information and establish a price for the company. The answer is not ignorance; every large organization has people who are familiar with the concept and successes of prediction markets, some who could champion an internal market as Fortune Elkins did at Misys (see chapter 9).

One obstacle is ingrained suspicion of the idea that lower-level employees might have input to management decisions. Senior managers value expertise, and when in doubt hire consultants. Another major obstacle is corporate culture (discussed in chapter 16).

After spending a year and a half researching this book, I have come to understand that there is a third reason. Managers may be aware of the issues, but just do not want to be faced with answers. The truth may set you free, but you may not want to hear it.

A classic example comes from the vice president of a company that provides prediction market software and solutions. Call it the Michael Corporation. In 2007, two Michael executives did a presentation to Chrysler Corporation in Auburn Hills, Michigan, on the virtues of launching a market to provide insight into a broad range of company issues. The presentation went well. Chrysler executives seemed intrigued.

Two days later, Michael received a two-line e-mail from Chrysler: "We do not wish to proceed with this. Thank you for your interest in Chrysler." One of the Michael vice presidents knew a Chrysler attendee from earlier employment; he called to ask what happened.

> "We thought the presentation went well."

> "It did; you were great, and the prediction market idea is promising."

> "So why the rejection?"

> "Do you really want to know? You identified many of the questions that a prediction market here could deal with, questions that need to be answered. But no one in that room wants them answered. The company couldn't handle the information."

I have paraphrased the conversation, but that is the general idea. In fairness to Chrysler, I later learned that Brian Wallace, manager of strategic planning for Chrysler, had encouraged the minivan division of the company to use Inkling markets for internal demand forecasting. One Chrysler prediction market involved the percentage mix of three available seat options: standard bench seats, stow-and-go, or swivel-and-go. The unwillingness to know was not companywide, or at least did not extend to design issues.

But consider what markets might offer an automotive company. Car companies typically run their proposed new auto designs through what they call a *car clinic*, an expensive focus group exercise using potential buyers. Prediction market company Crowdcast runs markets for General Motors, where engineers and supervisors are asked to predict a quantitative result: what the car clinic numbers will be. For competitive reasons, neither GM nor Crowdcast will talk about market outcomes, but if accurate (and GM continues to run them), this holds promise of major cost and time savings.

Not wanting to know holds true for successful companies as well as struggling ones. Consider the experience of the world's two largest aircraft manufacturers. Each knew about prediction markets, and each knew the cost of relying on imperfect information. Each decided not to use a market. The first company is Boeing, builder of the 787 Dreamliner, whose story was told in chapter 10. The second aerospace company is European Aeronautic Defence and Space (EADS), rival to Boeing and builder of the Airbus group of airliners. EADS announced in 2006 that it would build a new aircraft to compete with the 787 and would use a network of global suppliers comparable to that used by Boeing. The new Airbus was scheduled for 2012 delivery.

Prediction market enthusiasts waited to see whether EADS would embrace an internal market to track its own progress. It did not. EADS knew what Boeing might have learned from a prediction market; that was detailed in an internal EADS study titled *Boeing 787 Lessons Learned*. The cautionary tale of the Boeing delay, plus the earlier two-year delay in delivery of its own A380 superjumbo (which cost EADS €2 billion in penalties and lost profit) somehow did not provide enough motivation to start its own market.

Why would no one within EADS champion a prediction market? Why would no one want to know? In part, the explanation seems to have been the same taboo that worried Jeff Severts at Best Buy. It is inherently dangerous to question whether an initiative that is important to the corporation might fail. The more important the question, the more relevant the taboo. If Airbus were to ask, "When will we deliver the first plane?" and an employee and supplier-driven market might answer, "Eight months late," there are managers who would resist having the question asked. To even suggest an internal market posing such a question might be viewed as betrayal.

Why would senior management at EADS, or the board, not establish a top-down market? Perhaps the French-German management structure at the government-owned company was not receptive to bottom-up information. Or perhaps management was not interested in a market that might contradict the chairman's public position on meeting the delivery deadline.

One EADS executive suggested a tendency in European top management to what in US business schools is called the *WYSIATI* (what you see is all there is) bias. The executive mind builds a coherent narrative around a problem, basing it on the evidence available, and fills in the unknowns in the story according to its own experience and perceptions. A market-based result is thought to overcome the resulting bias by involving people with different experiences and perceptions. Biases in the original will be apparent to at least some participants, who will invest in favor of a different outcome.

EADS had another reason to embrace an early-warning market. At the time the company announced the new Airbus, EADS was well into development of its A440M military transport plane, the biggest defense procurement project in Europe. This project was also not going well. By the beginning of 2010, the company was already four years late for a test flight of the first A440M and €990 million ($1.25 billion) over budget.

The company had committed to test-fly the A440M by the end of March 2009. If it missed that deadline, EADS was subject to financial penalties of €1.7 billion ($2.12 billion). Customers had the right to cancel their orders and reclaim €5.7 billion ($7.1 billion) in deposits. If there were contract cancellations, customers would presumably order Lockheed Martin's established C-130 transport, or Boeing's C-17.

As with Boeing, the major problem with the Airbus A440M was out-side suppliers; in this case those designing and producing the engines. This was being done by a consortium of the French manufacturer Snecma, Britain's Rolls Royce, Spain's ITP, and Germany's MTU Aero Engines. EADS said it was unaware that engine production had fallen so far behind schedule.

The March test flight deadline was missed. Airbus negotiated a further three-month test-flight extension to coincide with the plane's exhibition at the Paris Air Show. Louis Gallois, the chief executive of EADS, insisted the new deadline could be met. One European prediction market, pre-sumably with participation from company engineers and those involved in engine design, suggested a 2 percent probability of the deadline being met. It was not.

The contract to exhibit at the Paris Air Show was canceled. A proto-type could have been displayed, but the absence of engines on the aircraft would have been conspicuous. The company then negotiated a further delay for the test flight and announced the plane would be flightwor-thy in the fall. Another commercial prediction market on that possibility opened at 15 cents, and rose steadily to 80 cents by the end of November. The plane did fly—although not very far—in mid-December 2009. EADS then announced the aircraft would require an additional three years of testing and 4,370 hours of flying before it could enter service.

There are other situations, not just within organizations, but across the economy, where a prediction market may have helped, but where no one seemed to want to know. The most dramatic example imaginable is the great credit crash of 2007, a blow to the world economic system that is still hard to comprehend. Over an eighteen-month period, US eq-uities lost 40 percent of their value, commercial real estate 40 percent, and housing a third. Many of these assets ended up with negative equity, meaning the value of the assets was lower than the value of the debt they carried. Owners walked away from homes and commercial buildings.

The total loss of perceived wealth was $20 trillion (twenty thousand billion dollars!) from a pre-crash total of $50 trillion. Bank failures were reported daily on the front page of newspapers. By the end of 2008, the

US Treasury and Federal Reserve System had committed two and a half trillion dollars to stabilize the financial system. The system did return more or less to normal, but with many of its leading players deceased, disabled, downsized, or under new ownership.

Financial crises are not rare. They are infrequent, but not random. They result from wild risk taking, excessive debt leverage, and regulatory failure. In the usual run-up, financial firms make record profits, regulators are content, and almost everyone chooses to ignore the risks.

But securities markets are supposed to be collectively smart, and certainly a few observers saw what was happening prior to 2007. So what went wrong? What happened is, there was an information cascade that caused investors both to act in unison and to make bad choices. This does not happen frequently, but it does happen. Those who manage investment firms are subject to "the country club effect." Investors sit around with friends, and everyone brags about their huge profits. The conversations change the way they think about risk, and lessen their anxiety that tomorrow will not be just like today. Investment firms want the same huge profits their competitors are said to be reaping.

The 2008 crash was caused by a lot of unusual things happening almost simultaneously. The most important was massive losses in collateralized debt obligations (CDOs) and other exotic financial instruments such as mortgage-backed securities. Did anyone see this coming? Would properly designed predictions markets have provided a warning? Would anyone have paid attention to a market? The answers are yes, yes, and probably no.

The first modern-day CDO was launched by US investment bank JP Morgan in 1998. It involved corporate loans rather than mortgages. JP Morgan pooled 307 corporate loans with a face value of about $10 billion, and sold shares in the pooled assets. Interest payments came from the income stream from the corporate loans. The underlying loans were all with companies rated triple-A by a major credit-ranking agency.

The attraction of CDOs was that pooling seemed to further minimize risk to the buyer of the security. One or two companies might default, but most would continue making interest payments. JP Morgan loved the CDO idea because, even if the securities defaulted, its share of the residual risk would be taken over by insurance company AIG, which was willing to insure subprime securities in return for trivial premiums. The cost of this insurance was only two-tenths of a cent per dollar per year. With AIG taking on the residual risk, JP Morgan only had to set aside $160 million as a reserve against each $10 billion of CDOs issued, rather than the $800 million it would have had to set aside against individual loans.

AIG also loved CDOs. At the beginning it earned a lot of money providing residual risk insurance. Two-tenths of a cent does not sound like much, but multiplied by 10 billion it produced $20 million in premiums a year. There were no defaults. JP Morgan earned a commission on sales and had its own capital freed up. Everyone made money. By the end of 1999, $100 billion in CDOs had been sold.

The problem with this everyone-wins scenario is what economists call *correlation*. JP Morgan and those who purchased its CDOs operated on the assumption that the chance of one corporate loan default was unrelated to whether other loans defaulted. But anyone who thought about it knew this could not be right. As we later saw, if Chrysler could not pay its bills, its suppliers would have major financial problems. The suppliers' unpaid and laid-off employees would buy less. Restaurants, building-supply dealers, and golf courses might then fail, taking some bankers with them.

If a long chain of defaults happened, neither AIG nor JP Morgan had enough money to pay off CDO holders. These securities were safer than the underlying loans only if there was no correlation in corporate debt defaults. If there was correlation, when the dollar value of outstanding CDOs increased, so did the potential loss.

Did investment banks know about the correlation problem? Of course. Within a year of issuing the first CDOs, JP Morgan cut back dramatically on the dollar value of the securities it was willing to hold. AIG responded to the perceived higher risk by raising its insurance rates by a factor of more than five, to one and one-tenth cents per dollar per year. Would a prediction market have indicated a concern with corporate-loan-based CDOs? Yes, if the market was made up of bankers or investors who understood the underlying no-correlation assumption.

As it cut back on corporate CDOs, JP Morgan began to build a new business in home mortgage–backed CDOs. This involved bundling thousands of residential mortgages and selling investors a mortgage-backed security. The interest payment on these CDOs came from the flow of mortgage payments from borrowers.

The great feature of this market for JP Morgan and other investment bankers was that while investors in corporate CDOs wanted to know the identity of the corporations behind the underlying loans, no one asked the names or credit histories of the homeowners who were making interest payments on mortgages. The mortgage-backed CDO market also offered a more profitable revenue model. Lots of money was to be made in bundling mortgages and selling the resulting securities. Further income came from managing mortgage payments and redemptions on behalf of the security holders.

JP Morgan (and the other investment banks involved in mortgage-backed CDOs) tried to diversify risk by bundling mortgage loans from different regions of the country. If Cleveland, Ohio, suffered a downturn, the theory was that Sacramento, California, would still be strong. But there was also a very real correlation risk with these securities. In a recession, unemployment rises, housing prices fall, and defaults increase everywhere. If mortgage failure risk was highly correlated across all regions of the country, then the billions of dollars in mortgage-backed securities imposed massive risk on the institutions that purchased them, and on anyone who guaranteed or insured them.

JP Morgan did understand the risk. The investment bank did four mortgage-backed CDOs. Then, as the quality rating of mortgages they were bundling dropped, they exited from the market. In late 2006, both JP Morgan and Goldman Sachs recognized the risks of the subprime mortgage market and developed financial products that would allow the firms to bet against mortgages with their own money and profit if residential mortgage prices weakened.

In the year before AIG's collapse and the government bailout, JP Morgan collected $7.2 billion from the insurer to compensate it for declines in value of various CDOs—and additional profits from shorting the shares of mortgage issuers.

To say the quality of the mortgages dropped is to understate the degree to which lending standards had cratered. At the very bottom of the crater was a mortgage instrument called an interest-only, negative-amortization, adjustable-rate subprime mortgage. Translated, that was a loan in which the new homeowner was given the option of making no mortgage payments, interest or principal, over a five-year period. The interest owed the lender, typically at 6 percent for the first two years and 11 percent thereafter, was rolled into a higher principal balance.

Who sought such a loan? Most were borrowers with no income. Loans were made to college students, new immigrants, and the long-term unemployed. You did not have to have an MBA in finance to see that danger lurked in this scenario.

A little above these—but only a little—were what was called *stated income mortgages*, also known as "liar" mortgages. Originators of these advertised that they would not require applicants to provide documentation of their supposed earnings. As long as investors were willing to buy packages of subprime mortgages, no questions were asked, supplying them guaranteed lavish short-term profits. Again, no MBA was required to predict the eventual outcome.

As JP Morgan dropped out of the mortgage-backed CDO market, other banks jumped in—on debt backed by mortgages, but also backed by things like monthly payments on cars. In 2006 alone, $500 billion in CDOs were sold.

Many people warned of the danger. As early as 2005, Warren Buffett called derivatives and their inherent risk, "weapons of mass destruction." Also in 2005, Michael Gelband, head of fixed income securities at Lehman Brothers, warned that aggressive mortgage lenders like Countrywide and New Century Financial had created $1 trillion in economic activity based on "false money," and were sure to fail. While one department of investment bank Lehman Brothers sold mortgage-backed CDOs, another

Lehman department sold short the shares of companies that issued the mortgages (selling those shares in the hope of buying them back later, at a lower price, when the price had fallen), and made a great deal of money. Meanwhile, the first Lehman department kept packaging and selling subprime mortgages.

In 2006, Richard Cayne Perry, founder of Perry Capital in New York and one of the most successful and influential investors of his time, proved immune to the country club effect and started shorting subprime mortgage securities. Perry was open about what he was doing; he recommended to anyone who would listen that they do the same. Few did. Perry went his own way, reportedly earning $1 billion in five months of shorting.

When the Securities and Exchange Commission investigated firms that had crashed they found a flood of cautionary internal e-mails. One senior manager wrote, "Lets [sic] hope we are all wealthy and retired by the time this house of cards falters."

Would a prediction market with the right question have highlighted the problem? Yes, if the market were made up of even moderately financially savvy investors. Would anyone have been motivated to set up and run such a prediction market? Probably not. Certainly not the investment banks, whose own shares would have tumbled if a market had concluded there was great risk. Would anyone willing to ignore a warning from Warren Buffett or Richard Cayne Perry have paid attention to a warning from an anonymous market?

Consider another disaster that became the subject of humor and scorn by commentators: the 2008 economic collapse and virtual insolvency of Iceland. Following a six-week financial implosion, the country had a national debt of eight and a half times its gross domestic product, $330,000 of debt for each of the 300,000 Icelanders. Its three national banks were insolvent and nationalized. Its currency, the krona, lost 70 percent of its value against the euro. Its stock market lost 82 percent of its value.

Many saw the Icelandic crash coming. As early as 2003, Copenhagen's Danske Bank issued a report that the Icelandic financial system was likely to fail. In January 2008, the hedge fund division of Bear Stearns convened a meeting of six other investment banks to discuss how money could be made from Iceland's pending collapse. Funds and individuals sold short Icelandic bank stocks and the shares of every other Icelandic institution they could find.

A few people tried to warn Icelanders, but most seemed not to want to hear. In May 2008, noted University of Chicago economist Robert Aliber gave a public lecture at the University of Iceland in Reykjavik, describing the Icelandic economy as a giant bubble. Aliber said, "I give you nine months. Your banks are dead. Your bankers are either stupid or greedy." An article in *Vanity Fair* later claimed that local bankers demanded that newspapers not report his comments. In any case, Aliber was wrong. It wasn't nine months. It was three.

A properly structured prediction market—and one open to foreigners—that had asked the right questions a year earlier might have helped save the Icelandic economy. A market taking place at the time of Aliber's talk would undoubtedly have highlighted what so many people already knew. At that point, a market result might just have created an earlier crash.

One obvious idea that flows from this chapter is the desirability of running markets in any organizational setting where informational or reputational cascades are frequent and mistakes are costly—think of Lehman or Boeing. A market would at least produce a public result that might mitigate the cascade, or that could be cited by anyone willing to stand in its path.

But what do you do in the case where an organization really does not want to know? Should a technology evangelist within the company risk starting a trial prediction market, start with innocuous questions, and slowly introduce more meaningful ones? Such a market might provide warning signals that a few will pay attention to, but a market without high-level cover might prove a career-limiting move for the evangelist.

16

More Red Flags Than Beijing

In today's regulatory environment, it's virtually impossible to violate rules. It's impossible for a violation to go undetected, certainly not for a considerable period of time.

—Bernard Madoff, legendary Ponzi investor

In the choice between changing one's mind and proving there's no need to do so, most people get busy on the proof.

—John Kenneth Galbraith, American economist

ONE OF THE GREAT head-in-the-sand tales of our time concerns Bernard Madoff, perpetrator of what has been called the biggest investor fraud of all time. Madoff is the man who brought the term *Ponzi scheme* back to public consciousness. In a Ponzi scheme, early investors in a scam are paid huge returns, not from the investment but with funds contributed by later investors. Charles Ponzi, whose exploits immortalized his name, was an early-twentieth-century con man who promised clients a 50 percent profit within forty-five days or 100 percent profit within ninety days—their choice. Ponzi said he was buying discounted postal coupons in other countries and redeeming them in the United States. The wonder of this scheme, as with later Ponzi schemes, is why anyone would accept a premise that was so improbable on its face.

On March 12, 2009, Madoff pled guilty to securities fraud and ten other counts of defrauding clients of almost $65 billion, more than half of which was later recovered. In his statement to the court, Madoff said that he had started his scheme in the 1990s, with the claim that huge profits would come from a "split-strike conversion strategy." He admitted that he had actually invested very little of his clients' money, but instead deposited the funds in his bank account and used the money to pay rates of return as high as 20 percent per year.

Michael Lewis, author of *Liar's Poker*, and David Einhorn, president of hedge fund Greenlight Capital, wrote a wonderful op-ed piece in the *New York Times* in January 2009. They illustrated the "head-in-sand, not wanting to know" attitude with the depressing story of Harry Markopolos, a man who spent several years of his career trying to out Madoff.

Markopolos was a respected investment officer with Rampart Investments in Boston. In 1999, Markopolos's boss became aware of Madoff's high investment returns and asked Markopolos to come up with a formula to duplicate them. Markopolos quickly realized the returns were mathematically impossible, given Madoff's stated strategy. For nine years, he tried to persuade both his boss and the Securities and Exchange Commission that Bernard Madoff had to be a fraud. Markopolos illustrated to each how the results claimed were impossible. Not difficult, not extreme, just mathematically impossible. Run the numbers against Madoff's declared strategy, he said—20 percent a year can't be done. Markopolos pointed out that Madoff reported only three loss months over more than seven years: "His returns were as reliable as the swallows returning to Capistrano."

Madoff's reported option transactions often exceeded the entire reported volume of exchange contracts for options with the same purchase date, strike price, and expiration date. Feeder funds for Madoff received statements that reported option transactions more numerous than the entire market for that option on that day. In short, there were not enough options in existence to provide the hedging that Madoff claimed as a key part of his strategy.

Thousands of trades were logged as taking place at prices outside the stock exchange's reported daily trading range. Madoff also showed trade tickets for stock transactions that supposedly took place on Saturdays and other nonworking days. Finally, Markopolos noted that Madoff employed a one-man accounting firm to audit his $50 billion empire.

In 2005, Markopolos sent the SEC a seventeen-page letter titled "The World's Biggest Hedge Fund Is a Fraud," in which he discussed two possible scenarios for Madoff's results. Markopolos later documented the whole nine-year adventure in a book, *No One Would Listen.*

In the first scenario in the SEC letter, Markopolos described Madoff, who also operated as an investment broker, as illegally front-running his brokerage clients. This means that when a customer asked Madoff to purchase a security, he bought it for his own portfolio. If the stock rose in value overnight, Madoff kept the stock and bought the customer a replacement at the higher price. If it dropped in value, he put the original security in the customer's account. Scenario number two was the Ponzi scheme, where high returns were paid from newly raised investor capital.

Markopolos says that many of Madoff's European investors knew he could not achieve his announced returns from a split-strike strategy; they accepted that he was front-running and that they were the beneficiaries. They did not look deeper to see if he was also cheating other clients.

Markopolos's missive landed on the desk of Meagan Cheung, Securities and Exchange Commission (SEC) branch chief in New York. Cheung signed off on a brief SEC investigation that "found no evidence of fraud." Markopolos later wrote of the "no evidence" conclusion, "With the materials we submitted, it would have taken investigators no more than the time it took to ask Madoff three questions for his fraud to be discovered and his operation to be shut down. The magnitude of this Ponzi scheme is matched only by the willful blindness of the SEC in investigating Madoff."

In June 2009, Madoff was sentenced to 150 years in prison. After the sentencing, Lori Richards, Cheung's superior and head of the SEC office that inspects money managers and brokerages, agreed to resign her position for failing to conduct an inspection of the money-management side of Madoff's business. Three months later, two defrauded investors sued the SEC and the US government for $1 billion, citing the finding of no fraud when, they said, there was abundant evidence to the contrary.

Markopolos was not even the first to express concern. From 1992 through 2008, the SEC received seven similar warnings. Each time, the agency concluded nothing was wrong. Two of the warnings were triggered by Madoff's refusal to let brokers or financial feeder funds perform due diligence on his fund. The French bank Société Générale issued a warning letter to clients in 2003, advising against the Madoff funds for the same reason Markopolos gave: the high level of reported returns over a long period of years could not be true.

HSBC Bank acted on warnings by outsiders and twice by its own executives in 2006 and 2008, by hiring accounting firm KPMG to look at Madoff's operations. Each time, KPMG presented a detailed warning of the "baffling and potential fraudulent returns of the fund." HSBC ignored both warnings and continued to act for feeder funds that directed money to Madoff. The trustee charged with recovering money for Madoff's victims filed a $9 billion claim against HSBC and other European institutions, alleging that ignoring these and other warnings constituted negligence. HSBC's position is that the claims are unfounded.

Would a prediction market have raised warning signals about Madoff? It is possible, given the right questions and informed investors. But would anyone regularly reassured by the SEC and the participation of major banks and enjoying 20 percent annual returns have run such a market? The warning would have to have been offered by a respected third party with an established history of accuracy.

These illustrations are all from the world of economics and finance. But willfully ignoring red flags is much more widespread. My favorite example comes from the august field of medicine. It involves ulcers, a condition familiar to many readers.

For most of the twentieth century, all physicians accepted that ulcers were caused by stress and lifestyle, and in particular by excessive consumption of alcohol and spicy foods. Every physician was taught this; no one questioned it. Treatment for ulcers included antacids, restricted diets, and surgical removal of the ulcerous part of the stomach. Up to 15 percent of patients died from the surgery.

In 1985, two Australian medical researchers, Barry Marshall and Robin Warren, spoke at a major medical conference in Brussels and reported that the lifestyle theory was wrong. Ulcers were caused, they said, by a humble bacterium, and were easily curable. The audience of physicians was incredulous and disbelieving; one called Marshall a madman: no bacterium could survive in the stomach's acid environment. Another hurled a balled-up program as the two left the podium.

Marshall and Warren's research had been both fortuitous and innovative. While conducting autopsies, Marshall had found a hitherto unknown bacterial species, later called *Helicobacter pylori*, present in the lower stomach in almost all patients with gastric inflammation, duodenal ulcer, or gastric ulcer. The bacterium was not present in patients without these conditions.

Marshall cultivated the bacterium in a Petri dish. He fed it to rats, but failed to produce rat ulcers. He then did what most researchers would never consider. He drank the contents of the Petri dish. Three days later he developed extreme gastritis. He took a short regimen of antibiotics and the symptoms disappeared. He tried antibiotics on his patients, and within weeks had eradicated symptoms in 80 percent of them. Solid proof? Never underestimate the message in the Galbraith quote at the beginning of the chapter: "In the choice between changing one's mind and proving there's no need to do so, most people get busy on the proof."

Marshall and Warren wrote up their research results and submitted them to the distinguished British medical journal *Lancet*. Their article was rejected. They rewrote it and submitted it to the more progressive *New England Journal of Medicine*. That article was rejected. Both sets of reviewers said that everyone knew that bacteria were not the cause of ulcers.

For almost twenty years following their report, many of Marshall and Warren's patients, and others in Australia and New Zealand, were cured of ulcers by a course of antibiotics and secretion inhibitors. In much of the rest of the world, it was diet and surgery. Several well-regarded British medical schools were teaching the lifestyle-causes-ulcers theory at the close of the twentieth century.

Why did the bacterium explanation have such a long path to acceptance? Marshall thinks it was because gastroenterologists and surgeons had a huge vested interest in what they already knew to be correct. They did not want to know that what they believed was not worth knowing. It took researchers who had no interest in the status quo, and new doctors who tried the antibiotic option and passed on the results by word of mouth, to change ulcer treatment.

Would a properly structured prediction market have signaled the right answer a decade earlier? Without question. Doctors who had great success with antibiotics and secretion inhibitors would have invested and reinvested in the answer they knew to be correct. But who was in a position to offer such a security? Would nonbelievers have been converted by a market signaling the correct answer?

In 2005, twenty years after they first announced their discovery, Barry Marshall and Robin Warren could only smile at the memory of being pelted by a balled-up program thrown by a disdainful doctor as they stood in the Royal Palace in Stockholm to receive the Nobel Prize in Medicine for their discovery of the role of a humble bacterium in peptic ulcer disease.

So how do you utilize a prediction market when there is an institutional culture firmly in the way? With either Madoff's returns or the use of antibiotics and secretion inhibitors, a properly structured market would have signaled the right answer. But such a market would have to be run by a respected group and open only to qualified professionals. Would any financial group or medical association have run it, against its own interests? Who else was in a position to offer it?

17

Finding the Scorpion

Of our departed shipmates still on patrol,
Let them know that we who survive,
Will always keep their memories alive.

—*The Submariner's Prayer*, author unknown

I F AN ESTIMATION MARKET can foretell the weight of a dressed ox, supply correct answers to *Who Wants to Be a Millionaire* questions, and predict temperatures, could it do the same for the cause and details of a disaster? Can there be a persuasive answer to a question when no investor in the market has more than a few bits of information? This is a cautionary tale about the need for skepticism when accepting the results of an elaborate prediction market—not only from an estimation market or from one on disasters, although those two provide great case studies.

Support for the idea that an appropriate market could spot the cause of a disaster came with the well-publicized stock market reaction to the space shuttle *Challenger* disaster. At 11:39 a.m. Eastern Standard Time on January 28, 1986, *Challenger* exploded 73 seconds after liftoff from Florida's Cape Canaveral. Twenty-five minutes later, NASA announced that *Challenger* was lost, but no commentator offered any details. However, the New York Stock Exchange, one of the largest possible prediction markets, identified the cause minutes after the tragedy and months before an investigative board issued its report.

There were four publicly traded major contractors involved in the shuttle launch program. Rockwell International produced the shuttle and its engines, Martin Marietta manufactured external fuel tanks, Morton Thiokol manufactured solid-fuel booster rockets, and Lockheed Martin provided ground support. As reported in a *Journal of Corporate Finance* article by Michael Maloney and Harold Mulherin, immediately after the explosion stock prices of all four companies fell between 3 and 6 percent. Trading was halted only for Morton Thiokol stock, which had a wave of sell orders without corresponding buy orders.

By the end of the trading day, Thiokol resumed trading with its share price down 12 percent from the previous day's high. The other three contractors were down 2 to 3 percent. Thiokol shares lost $200 million in market value in the twenty-four hours following the tragedy.

Over the next several months, the stocks of Rockwell, Martin Marietta, and Lockheed recovered their losses. Thiokol stock did not. The market treated Thiokol's stock as though that company was solely responsible for the disaster and would incur financial penalties.

In June 1986, five months after the explosion, a commission of inquiry chaired by former US secretary of state William Rogers issued a report blaming the *Challenger* disaster on defective O-ring seals on Thiokol's booster rockets. Following the report, NASA reached a financial settlement with Thiokol, which included penalties estimated to cost Thiokol about $200 million—almost exactly the decline in the company's equity value immediately following the tragedy.

Did Thiokol insiders realize what had happened and rush to sell their company stock? Maloney and Mulherin looked for this, as did investigators at the Securities and Exchange Commission. There was no insider selling. The drop in share price was seen as a reaffirmation of the idea that a market with many diverse investors reacts quickly and accurately to new information. *Challenger* became a textbook example that markets can predict the facts surrounding a disaster.

The most jaw-dropping prediction market story of all time, and perhaps the most important cautionary tale, involves a 1968 search in the North Atlantic for the missing US nuclear attack submarine *Scorpion*.

After months of searching, the sunken sub was located. A news story surfaced that this resulted from information from an elaborate prediction exercise run by US Navy scientist John Craven.

Craven and his predictors were said to have begun with no solid information about the sub's last location, direction, speed, or the nature of the fatal incident. Locating the sub through predictions from a group of relative amateurs was breathlessly described in James Surowiecki's *The Wisdom of Crowds* as "astonishing." It was cited in the *New York Times* and *BusinessWeek* as evidence of the wonders of markets. The story dominated presentations on prediction markets for two decades.

I and a hundred other business school professors have used the *Scorpion* story in executive courses and with grad students, complete with opaque references to how the search market worked. The tale always concluded that if a market could be used to locate a lost submarine with almost no information to work with, then carefully designed prediction markets had vastly greater potential than anyone had realized. No one at the time seemed to have looked behind the extraordinary headlines. Perhaps they should have.

John Craven is a worthy central character in such a tale. Craven is the great-grandson of Tunis Craven, commander of the Civil War ship *Tecumseh*, who drowned when his ship hit a mine laid by the Confederacy during the Battle of Mobile Bay (the sinking of *Tecumseh* inspired Admiral David Farragut's famous order, "Damn the torpedoes, full speed ahead"). John Craven was a prodigy; he entered high school at eleven and graduated at fifteen. When he turned seventeen, he applied to the US Naval Academy at Annapolis and was rejected. He attended Cornell and Caltech, earning a PhD in ocean engineering. He was project manager for the Polaris missile program, then was named chief scientist for the US Navy's Special Projects Office.

For fifteen years, Craven oversaw top-secret Cold War Navy projects. Prior to the search for *Scorpion*, his best-known use of decision theory involved finding a hydrogen bomb, lost from a United States B-52 bomber in January 1966, in deep water off Palomares, Spain. The aircraft, from the USAF Strategic Air Command, collided with a KC-135 tanker during midair refueling over the Mediterranean. Both planes were destroyed. The bomber carried four Mk 28 hydrogen bombs. Three were recovered on land; the fourth fell into the sea.

Decision theory could be applied to the lost hydrogen bomb because Craven knew the precise location of the midair collision, the speed and altitude of the aircraft, the air temperature, and the water depth. The missing variable was whether two, one, or no parachutes on the bomb had opened, and thus how far wind drift had carried the bomb. Craven ran a prediction exercise to determine the number of parachutes that had opened. He assigned probabilities to individual map-grid squares. The original search box was six miles (ten kilometers) by three miles (five kilometers). Craven's prediction group exercise was not complex, but the result was impressive. It cut the search box in half: five weeks' search time for a towed submersible.

On its tenth dive around Craven's "most likely" locations, the research sub *Alvin* sighted a single parachute covering a cylindrical object. The H-bomb was twenty-five hundred feet (seven hundred meters) underwater. The two-person *Alvin* crew tried to hook the parachute, but the bomb fell back into the sea. It was recovered three weeks later.

When *Scorpion* disappeared on May 22, 1968, half the US Navy's Atlantic fleet was tasked to find it. The search went on for five months. As the story is told, a month after the formal search ended, Craven again assembled a small group. This included a naval captain, a deckhand, a salvage expert, two mathematicians, and an oceanographer. Only two of the group had ever sailed on a nuclear sub.

Craven set up a market, asking questions in the form of wagers that would lead to identifying the sub's location. He used a standard statistical technique called Bayes Decision Theory to combine the estimates and pinpoint *Scorpion*'s final resting place. The technique, crafted by mathematician Thomas Bayes in 1702, describes what makes something "evidence," and assesses how much evidence it really is. Other statistical results are compared to the Bayes's method because it defines the maximum information you can extract from a given piece of evidence. Cognitive scientists use *Bayesian reasoner* as a code word for someone who demonstrates a highly rational reasoning process. It took a while for Bayes's approach to be accepted. He died in 1761; the formula was first published well after his death.

The spot Craven identified was a hundred miles (160 kilometers) from where the Navy had focused its search, and 90 degrees off the existing search line. The USS *Mizar* was sent to the location. Its camera sled spotted the sub 220 yards (200 meters) from the predicted spot, and 10,000 feet (3000 meters) down. The sub had broken in two, with parts scattered in two trenches over 330 feet (100 meters) of ocean bottom. No bodies or parts of the sub were ever brought to the surface.

Facts not in dispute are as follows. The USS *Scorpion*, launched in December 1959, was a Skipjack-class nuclear powered submarine, designed to find and sink enemy submarines and surface warships. In October 1968, *Scorpion* deployed to the Mediterranean to operate with the Sixth Fleet. On May 7, 1969, it was returning to its homeport at Naval Base Norfolk when it received orders to divert to a location just west of the Azores, to observe recently detected exercises by a small Soviet naval task force.

On May 21, *Scorpion* made its final radio contact with base. Thereafter, it did not acknowledge scheduled radio communications. The afternoon of May 22, the navy launched an informal search (meaning it was not announced publicly). On May 23, the Office of Naval Intelligence began a navy-wide search and seizure of all underwater listening device (Sound Surveillance System, or SOSUS) data and all *Scorpion* communication records. On June 5, *Scorpion* and her ninety-nine crew members were declared "presumed lost." The five-month search for the sub's final resting place followed.

Only the sub's position on the previous day was known. The search box for *Scorpion* at the time Craven began his process was 300 miles (500 kilometers) by 20 miles (30 kilometers)—thirty-three times the H-bomb search site, with almost no information to reduce the size of the box.

Craven is reported to have run his prediction exercise with a series of wagers involving different scenarios for what had happened to *Scorpion*. The variables included how far and in what direction the submarine traveled after its last radio communication, how deep the sub was when the incident happened, how the captain would have reacted to the emergency (did he attempt to blow the ballast tanks and surface?), and the sub's angle of descent to the ocean floor after the incident. The key variable was what happened to the sub. This is a classic example of how you might break down a complex problem into elements that could be entrusted to a market.

Participants in Craven's exercise were not allowed to consult each other before offering opinions on each variable. The participant with the most accurate wagers for each question, measured by the group's consensus result, was to receive a bottle of Chivas Regal scotch whisky.

Basing the prize on a group consensus is an example of what economist John Maynard Keynes called a "beauty contest." Keynes used the example of a 1920s *New York Times* newspaper competition in which entrants were asked to choose the six prettiest female faces from a hundred photographs. The prize went to the entrant whose choice most closely matches the majority choice of the other entrants. Keynes said an entrant would consider not beauty but, "Who will other judges think the most beautiful?" Every other entrant would ask the same question; the right approach is to pick the six faces that one thinks that others think, that others think (and so on), are the prettiest. Keynes said investing in the stock market was a beauty contest. A canny investor chose not what he thought was the best stock, but the stock he thought other investors would choose as best, thus driving up its price.

In the *Scorpion* case, each member of the group predicting the sub's location was really being asked not how far the sub had traveled, but rather how far each thought the others would say the sub had traveled: "What will other judges conclude?" Craven then weighted the results from individual wagers according to his perception of the expertise of each person, pulled the group consensus together, and predicted the sub's resting place. How the latter two steps were performed was never explained. It was later revealed that the consensus location announced by Craven was not even close to the prediction of any individual member of the group. In other words, no group member envisioned the same scenario for *Scorpion*'s fate as the one announced.

Logic suggests that Craven must have known the approximate location of *Scorpion* in advance of the experiment. Evidence for this conclusion came with the later release of the seized underwater SOSUS data, and information from listening stations in the Canary Islands and Newfoundland. Hydroacoustic tabulation systems, first developed to locate splashdown sites for Polaris and Russian ballistic missile tests, could have determined a search-circle for *Scorpion* only about a mile (1.6 kilometers) in diameter. One American surface vessel and eleven Soviet naval ships, including two submarines, were in reasonable proximity to where *Scorpion* sank. Their acoustic listening devices would have produced an accurate location for any submerged explosion or hull breakup.

Had the *Scorpion* sinking been accidental, Russian Navy officials could be expected to have relayed information about the location to the US Navy, if only to emphasize that they were not involved. Military affairs reporter Ed Offley, author of the controversial 2007 book *Scorpion Down: Sunk by the Soviets, Buried by the Pentagon*, says that the Soviet Navy did report to Moscow exactly where the sub had gone down. The US learned the location when it intercepted and decoded Soviet naval communications.

Why would the US Navy not want to admit it knew *Scorpion*'s location, and instead run an exhaustive five-month pseudo-hunt many miles from the actual location? There are four theories as to what happened to the submarine, two of which might explain such a choice.

The first theory is the "hot-running torpedo" or internal explosion. This was the navy's first official explanation. This theory says that two volatile chemicals that powered *Scorpion*'s Mark-3 conventional torpedoes accidently mixed to generate enormous heat, causing the torpedo to explode within the sub's firing tube. A second theory posits an explosion of one of *Scorpion*'s 250-pound batteries. Either event would have produced catastrophic flooding of the control room and midships compartments. The United Kingdom and the Soviet Union are each thought to have lost a sub to one of these problems. The August 2002 sinking of the Russian nuclear submarine *Kursk* by what was concluded to be a hot-running torpedo received extensive news coverage.

The third theory is the rogue torpedo. This came to light when the report of a naval court of inquiry on the sinking was declassified by the Clinton administration in 1993. According to this theory, a battery-powered acoustic homing torpedo began running within the sub's firing tube. Jettisoned from the tube, the torpedo automatically armed itself and began a search for an acoustic signature. The nearest engine noise would have been from *Scorpion.* Such an accident would have required a second failure—of a system that enabled the captain to deactivate the torpedo before it engaged the mother sub. The court of inquiry report said the rogue torpedo theory was championed by John Craven. The *Findings of Fact* did not endorse this theory, but listed it first among possible causes of loss.

The fourth and most controversial explanation, discussed in two recent books on the loss of *Scorpion*, was that an Echo II hunter-killer sub from the Soviet naval group tracked *Scorpion* and sank it. One version is that this was done with prior approval of Soviet Navy headquarters and presumably of a Politburo-level official. Another theory is that the Soviet government was not told.

It is argued that the sinking was simple retaliation for the sinking, eleven weeks earlier, of the Soviet Golf-II ballistic missile submarine *K-129* by the submarine USS *Swordfish* 300 miles (560 kilometers) off Pearl Harbor. There are two versions of that story. One is that *Swordfish* inadvertently rammed the Soviet sub, which carried three nuclear ballistic missiles, during antisubmarine warfare exercises. The second is that *Swordfish* nudged *K-129* into a sudden turn and dive that resulted in a collision with an undersea mountain. The maneuver, which US Navy tactical manuals call "shouldering," is used as a last resort to alter the course of an enemy sub that is too close to a US missile-carrying "boomer." When *Swordfish* docked in Yokosuka, Japan, two weeks after the loss of *K-129*, it was noted that the sub had a badly damaged sail and periscope. *Swordfish* Captain John Rigsbee explained that the sub had brushed a small iceberg in the Sea of Japan.

In support of the hostile action theory, Ed Offley cites classified SOSUS recordings documenting the presence of a second submarine in the vicinity of *Scorpion*, interpreted as the Echo II, and a SOSUS tape that experts said showed "inarguably" the sound of high-speed torpedo screws. Others have pointed out that the hostile action theory would explain the long delay in locating *Scorpion*. There would have been concern that hull damage would show an implosion rather than an explosion. As it turned out, the extent of damage permitted no determination.

In his book, Offley says that he was unable to obtain confirmation from former Soviet Navy submarine flag officers that they had sunk *Scorpion*, but there were many hints that that was exactly what had happened. Related information comes from author and retired US naval captain Peter Huchthausen, who interviewed retired Soviet admiral Viktor Dygalo. The admiral is reported as saying that the real story would never be revealed because there was an informal agreement between the two countries' senior naval officers to stop any further investigation into the losses of *Scorpion* and *K-129*. Huchthausen quotes Dygalo, "Forget about ever resolving these sad issues for the surviving families."

Given the level of Cold War tension at the time, it would have been a serious blow to US-Soviet relations for US President Lyndon Johnson to accuse the Soviet Navy of intentionally sinking an American nuclear submarine.

If the prediction market version of finding *Scorpion* is indeed accurate, then John Craven must rank as one of the patron saints of markets. If the navy already knew where *Scorpion* lay, then, given his senior status and access to classified information, John Craven likely was informed. If so, this most famous and cited of prediction market experiments may just have been Craven finding an innovative use for a market—to conceal from the Russians that the United States had broken their naval code and to bring closure to a tragedy while simultaneously easing Cold War tensions.

Either way, it is a great story, but one to be read as a cautionary warning of the importance of exercising skepticism when faced with the results of an opaque prediction market.

18

Becoming an Oracle

I would never have seen it had I not believed it.

A point of view can be a dangerous luxury when substituted for insight and understanding.

—Marshall McLuhan, cultural guru

WHY DON'T PREDICTION MARKETS have more universal acceptance in situations where people *do* want to know? There are a few cases where markets have been tried and met with little support. Few people know of these instances, so that is not the answer. Some research is required to understand best practices for running a market, but a smart tech employee could solve that problem in a week. Beyond the implementation issues are problems of corporate culture and problems of people.

The most intractable problem involves convincing executives that their own professional worth is in no way dependent on always having the right answer, on being the smartest person in the room. How do you get someone to adopt the mantra of Jim Lavoie and Joe Marino, "We freely acknowledge that we are not the two smartest people in the company. . . We've got a vision of where we want this thing to be at some point in time. But exactly how to get there, and what technologies to use, and how we should employ them—that is much bigger than any two people should be responsible for." How do you get executives to want to access the knowledge and insight of junior colleagues?

My suggestion is to use the Jeff Severts's Best Buy experience (chapter 8) as a template. A technology evangelist starts a prediction market, first securing air cover from top management. This evangelist emphasizes to everyone who will listen that markets are not intended to replace executive knowledge or prerogatives, or the role of company experts.

Every time a corporate market is considered, the initiator also has to consider who might be embarrassed by the question asked or the information disclosed. For a corporate market to take root, the single most important proviso may be that no middle-level manager should feel threatened by the existence of the market or what it might reveal. Recall the sequence of steps Severts took to move Best Buy's TagTrade market project forward. He started small, and started within his own functional area.

It is not just operating managers who feel threatened. Markets challenge existing prerogatives. Leslie Fine, chief scientist of Crowdcast, says that even where top managers accept the need for better information and embrace markets, and lower-level employees sign on enthusiastically, it is often middle managers who become the major barrier to implementation: "Middle managers fear anything that threatens the status quo information flow in the organization."

That also applies to managers of staff functions. Professional forecasters and any others who view a prediction market as a threat to their own fiefdoms will certainly resist. Why would they encourage the view that their function can be replaced by a fun Internet exercise?

At the beginning, it is necessary to downplay rather than oversell a new market. Even then, unless there is ongoing and enthusiastic air cover from the top as with Google or Best Buy, or unless markets can be positioned as just another tool, like marketing research, market advocates may not be willing to risk their careers to fight the fight.

Getting support means going beyond the simple management claim that "of course we encourage disagreement and reward challenges to the status quo." Michael Giberson from the business school at Texas Tech University maintains that saying, "Challenge the status quo," is the status quo. If that principle were followed, information would already flow smoothly within the organization and there would be no need for a market.

Even with the best effort to avoid embarrassment, at some point a troublesome answer will surface, and the market manager will have to think through how to handle the results. The manager must be prepared to state publicly, "Only 10 percent of our investors think the first Boeing 787 will be delivered on time," or "Only 40 percent of employees think customer centricity will justify its costs." Challenging the CEO's pet project may mean that investors abandon the sinking market, and the market manager drowns.

To maintain interest in the market, those who take part need to know that their opinions make a difference and are not going to be buried. They have to be told the outcome and told who won the T-shirts. This means the market manager must anticipate the implications of being the one to publicize that information.

Another concern, much more important than it first seems, is to be careful about asking fun questions. Stick to "Who will win the NBA Finals?" If a market poses a question on a topic about which investors have no relevant knowledge, investors will try to answer. The market will produce meaningless results and both management and investors will lose interest. Try asking any group you can assemble—PhDs, six-year-olds, or clairvoyants—to predict the winning number in next week's lottery. Asking passengers about to board a Boeing 777 at Heathrow to predict the best flight route into Kennedy Airport is unlikely to improve on the expert judgment of the navigator. Where there is little or no information to aggregate, prediction markets become guessing markets, and investors give them the same momentary attention granted a telephone survey-taker.

A less obvious form of garbage-in, garbage-out, but one even more likely to leave a negative view of prediction markets, is the offering of fun markets on public events that have generated lots of media chatter but little transparency as to how decisions are made. When the event being predicted is decided in secret by a lone decision maker or a small group who never reveal their criteria, the prediction process often fails amid loud chuckling by market skeptics.

In most cases, low-transparency markets just follow media predictions. Consider the Intrade market on whether Moscow, New York City, Madrid, Paris, or London would host the 2012 Summer Olympics. The Paris security led for the entire market period, closing at a price reflecting a 63 percent chance of victory. Those who did invest probably got their insights from newspaper articles, television sportscasters, or blogs. London won, with Paris reportedly a close second, perhaps just proving how little the public knows about the decision process of the International Olympic Committee.

For years, Intrade ran markets on the capture or death of Osama bin Laden, but the market did not anticipate his April 2011 death at the hands of US SEAL Special Forces. The day before the event, the Intrade market was predicting a 3.8 percent chance that bin Laden would be killed or neutralized in the six-month period to September 2011—the tenth anniversary of 9/11. The market had been stable at 3–4 percent for weeks. Trading was thin, and market volume low.

Why was this long-running market wrong? The Intrade investments were probably an aggregation of speculation and wishful thinking. Market participants had little information on which to make an informed decision. Those who did know—the SEAL officers, the assault team, and those in the White House Situation Room—were high-ranking, sworn-to-secrecy, and unlikely to log on to Intrade.

A more interesting question is whether markets considered bin Laden's death important. Before the bin Laden event, the Intrade market on President Obama's 2012 reelection was trading at 58 percent. News of the killing caused daily trading volume in this market to double, and the price to soar to 70 percent overnight. The Obama reelection price dropped back to 62 percent the next day, and 59 percent two days later. The market quickly reached the same opinion as Nobel Prize–winning economist Paul Krugman, who said of the event, "It is hard to see that it changes anything important."

Often concerns about launching a prediction market take the form of restating the perceived shortcomings. These mirror the problems cited by skeptical newspaper columnists: executives will cheat, markets will have too few investors, trading volumes will be too small, rewards will not be significant enough to motivate good decision making, or investors don't have useful information to bring to the market. A few of these will be raised in any discussion on creating a company prediction market.

When a new market is launched, will a manager pressure subordinates to invest so as to mask what is actually going on or rig the market in some other way? It is easy to rationalize that a manager really should want to have early warning rather than miss a deadline or a product launch later. But he also might decide to try to avoid negative information now and hope for a miracle to rescue the project. Once a market is established and has management support, it is difficult to rig, if only because pressuring subordinates to lie may be too public and too demeaning. If trading is anonymous, pressuring is just not effective. If anyone tries manipulation, as long as there is enough liquidity in a market, other traders will correct the imbalance.

How about including market insiders? One concern is that for many questions asked in a corporate market, there are employees who have worked on that problem and possess inside information. We want them to invest—the market is there to assemble good information. If insiders are not allowed to trade, how much information do you lose? Think again of Boeing's 787 (chapter 10).

The related concern is whether the market manager wants individuals to betray the team effort and invest against the metrics of the project they have worked on. The answer is yes, if they believe "against" is the valid investing position.

Will markets have too few investors or trading volumes too small to motivate good decision making? Intrade and IEM's good results suggest small markets are enough. Markets run by Misys, Best Buy, and Google perform well with only a few hundred investors.

Many of the objections about too few market participants come from those who have taken a college statistics or survey research course. A basic rule for running a survey is that there must be many respondents, and they must be representative of the population. It is hugely counterintuitive that a small number of self-selected people can possibly produce good predictions.

Most markets use play money or offer prizes of small monetary value. This leads to the argument that such markets must falter. The concern is apparent to anyone who has played table poker for quarters or online poker with play money. Low stakes encourage sloppy play; players stay in with bad hands.

But again and again in the cases I've cited in this book, play-money markets generate predictions as accurate as those coming from real-money markets. These markets attract traders with recognition, other ego rewards, and the promise of an input to important decisions. The Misys and Google examples suggest that a T-shirt identifying the winner may be enough.

Sports markets also provide support for the idea that play money produces good predictions. A study by Emile Servan-Schreiber and others showed that the NewsFutures play-money exchange performed just as well as TradeSports.com, a real-money market, on a whole season's worth of National Football League predictions. Each market attracted an average of 200 investors per game. How good was their predictive accuracy? In a ranking against 1,947 human predictors on predictions covering the same 208 NFL games, the NewsFutures and TradeSports predictions ranked eleventh and twelfth.

For all the human and organizational hurdles involved in establishing a prediction market, those who have done it say that it really is worth doing. Markets can substitute for endless meetings, replace surveys, change an organization, and change society. Markets are usually the best aggregators of dispersed information, and certainly best at removing the filters that distort information as it moves higher in an organization.

The ultimate question is, do companies that have adopted prediction markets consistently make superior decisions to those that have not? The best evidence we have is that companies that begin to use prediction markets, *keep* using them—suggesting that the answers markets provide are thought to improve on whatever was used previously. The only companies I know of that have used markets and then dropped them are those where a market was introduced with insufficient explanation and caution, resulting in initial middle-management resistance. The other situation is where the predication market evangelist leaves, as with Fortune Elkins and Misys (see chapter 9), and no one steps up to take over.

The best intuitive evidence of market value comes with a Jim Lavoie quote: "Getting as many employees (current and past) to think about the future of the company is the key to optimizing your company's intellectual bandwidth in a knowledge economy, and to a feeling of enhanced personal relevance for every employee that participates. I pray my competition continues to rely on the corner office's *Wisdom of One.*"

In doing presentations on markets, I like to conclude with examples of really, really bad decisions by individuals who thought it necessary to be the smartest guy (they were all male) in the room. A few of my favorites appeared at the beginning of earlier chapters. Some, particularly those in the entertainment field, came to light when someone made a better prediction—otherwise we would never have known how shortsighted the original prediction was. The bad military predictions were not quickly rectified, and proved costly.

From the world of technology, this was offered in 1878 by Erasmus Wilson, an eminent Oxford University professor:

> Ignore electric light. When the Paris Exhibition closes, electric light will close with it and no more be heard of.

A generation later, in 1898, Lord Kelvin, president of the British Royal Society, concluded:

> Don't waste time on foolish ideas. Radio has no future, X-rays are clearly a hoax, and the aeroplane is scientifically impossible.

In 1923, investors responding to David Sarnoff's request for money to develop radio concluded:

The wireless music box has no imaginable commercial value.
Who would pay for a message sent to no one in particular?

From the world of entertainment, we have Harry Warner, president of
Warner Brothers Studios, rejecting a new technology with the wisdom:

Who wants to hear actors talk?

In 1944 a modeling agency manager rejected Marilyn Monroe. His
suggestion:

You'd better learn secretarial skills or else get married.

Ten years later, in 1954, a concert manager fired Elvis Presley after one
performance, with the advice:

You ought to go back to driving a truck.

The following March, entertainment magazine *Variety* wrote off both
Presley and his music, concluding as to the future of rock and roll:

It will be gone by June.

And seven years after that, in 1962, the chief executive of Decca records wrote off the Beatles with the observation:

Groups of guitars are on the way out.

These are fun but not history-changing. Consider two military predictions, each of which had profound implications for the fate of the forces
involved. The first comes from Napoleon Bonaparte in 1800, after sitting
through a demonstration by Robert Fulton of how steamboats could be
used by the French Navy. He declared:

What, sir, would you make a ship sail against the wind and
currents by lighting a bonfire under her deck? I pray you,
excuse me, I have not the time to listen to such nonsense.

Field Marshall Sir Douglas Haig was chief of staff of the British
Expeditionary Force in World War I. Haig was later judged the worst-

performing general of that war. In 1916, his aide-de-camp, after viewing a demonstration of the new military tank the German Army was using to devastate British and French cavalry units, wrote a report that Haig signed off on. It concluded:

> The idea that cavalry will be replaced by these iron coaches is absurd. It is little short of treasonous.

Field Marshall Haig was notoriously and maniacally pro-cavalry. An informal prediction exercise rather than the informational and reputational cascade triggered by his aide-de-camp might have resulted in several hundred thousand fewer British casualties.

My favorite example of an unnecessarily bad decision is literary, but it perfectly illustrates the need to get the best possible information from as many sources as possible. In the best-selling novel *Jurassic Park*, Michael Crichton describes an expert paleontologist who loudly claims and firmly believes that *Tyrannosaurus rex* has such bad eyesight that it will respond only to rapid movements by its prey. Finding himself trapped in an enclosure with a T. rex, the expert stands perfectly still. The T. rex eats him.

A few chapters later, someone asks what killed the man. "He was misinformed."

Postscript and Acknowledgments

The prophets are silent now; oracles stay away from Earth; Go!
Delphic flock, look for gods in another place.

— Johannes Kepler, Eulogy for Tycho Brahe (1601)

My own interest in the subject of prediction markets did not start with the tale of Francis Galton's ox or with Surowiecki's *The Wisdom of Crowds*, but it was certainly tweaked by each. Surowiecki's book only touches on prediction markets; it explores a fascinating mix of cognitive and other examples of groups sharing collective intelligence and producing accurate answers. Surowiecki's title is a reference to Charles MacKay's skeptical 1841 classic, *Extraordinary Popular Delusions and the Madness of Crowds*. MacKay cited the herd mentality that led to the Dutch tulip bubble in the 1630s and other disasters, and concluded, "Men, it has been well said, think in herds. It will be seen that they go mad in herds, and only recover their senses slowly, and one by one." Galton argued otherwise.

My interest grew during a three-year stay in Turkey from 2003 to 2006; I was teaching in a graduate business program at Bilkent University in Ankara and working with the Turkish government. Business executives asked, "How can we do marketing research in Turkey when so many of our customers just look to buy what they think is fashionable in Italy?"

A fashion designer in Milan, a software company in California's Silicon Valley, or a builder of luxury automobiles in Germany gain insights from focus groups and other techniques utilizing a sophisticated consumer base. But how does a firm in Istanbul collect useful market research information in these categories?

The prediction market approach was promising. A market used this way is of course a beauty contest—not, "What shoe design will you wear next season?" but, "What shoe design will other Turkish women want to be wearing next season?"

Turkish government officials struggled with the details of a peace initiative for Cyprus that would be acceptable to both Turkish and Greek governments. One approach was a prediction market designed to break down the conditions of the Annan Plan, recommended in 2004 by Kofi Annan, then secretary general of the United Nations. The market initiative, unfortunately never given much consideration by Greek Cypriot negotiators, would have predicted what single or conditional changes would have to occur in the Plan terms to produce acceptance by each side. The Turkish Cypriot side had reluctantly accepted the Annan provisions as they were; the Greek Cypriot side rejected them. It was assumed the Turkish side would have to make further concessions to gain Greek acceptance. The idea was that officials on each side might reveal through a market what they could not discuss publicly.

The Cyprus problem was one that went beyond uncertainty. It wasn't possible to even estimate probabilities of different approaches being accepted. It was not even clear what all the alternatives were. Diplomats were faced with unknown unknowns. Aggregated judgment, however speculative, would have been helpful to both sides (or so we argued).

On a somewhat less serious level, I created a simple prediction market to prove to a group of 310 skeptical Turkish MBA and undergraduate business students that the market concept would be a more effective research tool than surveys or focus groups. Half of my twenty-seven market questions involved obscure knowledge, analogous to *Who Wants to Be a Millionaire*: "In what community is the Turkish camel wrestling festival held?" (yes, that is people wrestling camels—which have a nasty bite). Half the market involved predictions: "Name the winner of the 2005 Academy Award for best actress in a leading role." The prize was giant cookies for the winning group, plus my praise of their efforts.

Three students tied the collective result in the obscure fact section. Three different individuals tied the collective result for predictions. All

310 participants did worse than the collective result in the two categories combined. My Turkish students were convinced that prediction markets would work in their culture.

This book reflects collective knowledge from the individuals and organizations mentioned in the various chapters and thanked below. My previous books have reflected my own investigations; this one reports the genius of those who for a decade have run markets, thought about them, and written about them. I am grateful to all those who provided insights.

My first debt is to a group of highly innovative academics and researchers. The reader looking for further material on prediction markets can do far worse than enter "Robin Hanson" or "Justin Wolfers" into Google Search. Hanson is recognized as the father of prediction markets and is one of the most innovative thinkers in the field. He is responsible for many of the ideas and technologies that are now standard. He is a professor at George Mason University in Fairfax, Virginia, chief scientist at Consensus Point, and a research associate at the Future of Humanity Institute at Oxford University. Justin Wolfers teaches at the Wharton School, University of Pennsylvania.

Other academics whose work has informed me are, in alphabetical order, Michael Abramowicz at George Washington University; Robert Forsythe at the University of South Florida; Robert Hahn at Illinois Institute of Technology; M. Todd Henderson at University of Chicago Law School; John Ledyard at Caltech; Saul Levmore at University of Chicago Law School; Paul Milgrom at Stanford; Forrest Nelson, Joyce E. Berg, and Tom Rietz at the University of Iowa; Eric Snowberg at Stanford; Paul Tetlock at Yale School of Management; Philip E. Tetlock at University of California, Berkeley; Hal Varian at University of California, Berkeley (at the time of writing on leave as chief economist at Google); and Eric Zitzewitz at Dartmouth.

Cass Sunstein writes fascinating articles and books on how groups produce knowledge, including *Infotopia: How Many Minds Produce Knowledge*. Sunstein is Felix Frankfurter Professor of Law at Harvard Law School. At the time this book was written, he was on leave as President

Obama's "one-man think tank," with the formal title of Director of the Office of Information.

Among popular writers, always interesting are James Surowiecki and Tim Harford. Surowiecki writes in *Slate*, and has a regular column in *The New Yorker* magazine. Tim Harford writes *The Undercover Economist* column for the *Financial Times*, and in *Slate*. Worth following is *Mercury's Blog*, written by Chris F. Masse (www.blog.mercury-rac.com).

My thanks to others who contributed more directly to the insights in this book: Norris Clark, NewsFutures; Bo Cowgill, a doctoral candidate at University of California, Berkeley (on leave from Google); Fortune Elkins, Oracle (formerly with Misys); Leslie Fine, Crowdcast (formerly with Hewlett-Packard); Mat Fogerty, Crowdcast; Tom Gruca, University of Iowa; Brian Jaedike, Best Buy; Chris Hibbert, Zocalo; Jim Lavoie, Rite-Solutions; Rami Levy, Motorola; A. K. Pradeep, NeuroFocus; Linda Rebrovick, Consensus Point; and Alexander Ross, Long Bets Foundation.

A special thanks and farewell to John Delaney, a pioneer of commercial prediction markets and CEO of Intrade. John passed away in May 2011. He was climbing Mount Everest and had made it to within fifty meters of the summit when he collapsed. He was never to know that his wife had given birth to a daughter a few days earlier; she was christened Hope.

Each person mentioned contributed to the originality of my writing. As always, I use the term in the spirit of the comment by American Laurence J. Peter, author of *The Peter Principle*; originality is the art of remembering what you hear but often forgetting where you heard it.

Ed Dubrovsky, Rondil Gosine, Josephine Hsing-Ju Chen, Daniel Rattner, and Jianhua Yu contributed to the book during their graduate work at the Schulich School of Business at York University in Toronto. Galen McEnaney read the manuscript with an engineer's eye, and provided many suggestions to improve clarity.

Celia Hayley, my London editor, contributed insights on chapter sequencing, logic, and the case examples. It is always humbling to see the gaping holes Celia finds in a manuscript that I send her in the belief that it is already perfect.

My continuing great debt, as with previous books, is to my partner Kirsten Ward, for her support through the disappointments and rants of the writing process. Kirsten is a talented editor and critic; the extent to which this book is readable is largely the result of her comments on successive drafts.

Sincere thanks also to my editor Tim Sullivan and his colleagues Stephani Finks, Erica Truxler, Audra Longert, Allison Peter, Monica Jainschigg, and Kevin Evers at Harvard Business Review Press.

Finally, I acknowledge my debt to a source that few authors seem to mention: Google. The contribution goes beyond the Google examples in the book. Without Google's instant search capability, *Oracles* would have taken eight times as long to write and been much less comprehensive. How did writers function before the creation of that wonderful, prediction-market-based search engine? Thank you, Sergey Brin and Larry Page. Thank you, Andy Bechtolsheim, a cofounder of Sun Microsystems who provided the early-stage financing to Brin and Page. Thank you, Kleiner Perkins and Sequoia Capital, the firms that provided the second-stage venture capital. Each correctly predicted that Google was a transformational idea in its early form.

The sections that follow are principally intended for those readers who might want to take part in a prediction market, or to start one. The next section discusses the legal conundrum facing markets in the United States; I have referred to this situation throughout the book. Following that is a checklist for getting a market started, followed by a listing of available prediction market software, and a list of a few public prediction markets worth following. A bibliography of relevant readings concludes the book.

The Legal Conundrum Facing
US Prediction Markets

Every US state prohibits all gambling except for activities that are explicitly permitted by statute—like pari-mutuel horse race betting. *Gambling* is defined as an activity by which the house takes its profit in the form of a percentage of the money bet. This definition would not include play-money prediction markets or internal company markets with nominal prizes. It would technically apply to a real-money market such as the Iowa Electronic Markets, except that IEM is regulated by the government's Commodity Futures Trading Corporation (CFTC). This registration removes it from the category of gambling.

In spite of CFTC regulation, at least one state has threatened action against the University of Iowa. In 2000 the IEM offered a contract on Hillary Clinton's being elected to the US Senate from New York. The New York Attorney General asked his Iowa counterpart to file charges against the IEM. When Iowa declined to respond, he said his office would bring charges against any New York resident who traded on the IEM—not against anyone who invested in the Clinton security, but rather against anyone who traded any IEM security, ever.

George Neumann, then a University of Iowa business school professor and IEM board member, wrote to inform the New York District Attorney's office that the Iowa market possessed a CFTC exemption, meaning that the university, the school, and market participants were shielded from state-initiated criminal suits. The New York Attorney General's office never indicated whether it agreed or disagreed with this interpretation, but it ceased communicating and has taken no action against any IEM investor.

Even where they operate with real money and take a percentage of what is invested, prediction markets are very different from the usual concept of gambling. A prediction market produces a link between the money invested and the quality of the resulting prediction. Playing slot machines, spinning roulette wheels, tossing dice, or betting on the outcome of a horse race creates no resulting social benefit. This may sound like a convincing defense for the use of markets; however, no state or federal court has ever recognized the social benefit distinction.

Since prediction markets take place on the Internet, they may be covered by other federal laws, in particular the Unlawful Internet Gambling Enforcement Act, signed in 2006 by President George W. Bush. This was aimed at ending all Internet gambling originating within the United States, or directed at US residents.

The CFTC has investigated Intrade and TradeSports.com, each of which offered markets in the United States and used real money, but were physically located in Ireland—a jurisdiction where most forms of gambling are legal. Each organization argued that it was a kind of commodity market. In the past their location, more than the commodity market argument, had shielded them from US legal scrutiny. The CFTC enquiry focused not on the use of real money, but rather on the fact that TradeSports.com offered markets on the outcome of sporting events.

In 2006, the CFTC accepted an offer to settle from Trade Exchange Network (TEN), the parent company of Intrade and TradeSports.com. TEN did not admit that gambling had been involved, but agreed that the organizations had offered options contracts to US residents contrary to CFTC rules. TEN agreed that it would not offer contracts in the United States, would inform its US investors that TEN's markets were no longer available to them, and would pay a civil penalty of $150,000. In 2006, two years after the settlement, TradeSports.com ceased operation.

As part of the settlement, the CFTC agreed that Intrade could operate in the United States only with institutional participants or with individuals who met a high-net-worth test. The contracts Intrade offers must also be "unlikely to be susceptible to manipulation."

This may or may not have sheltered Intrade and its executives from CFTC action. Intrade CEO John Delaney said in a July 4, 2008, letter to the CFTC that "It is perversely unclear as to whether Intrade, and indeed myself, are considered persona gratis by the United States." Delaney said he had concerns about returning to the United States; his much-republished comment to reporter John Stossel of MSNBC was that "I don't look good in an orange jumpsuit."

There may be some basis for his concern. After the 2006 Gambling Act made all Internet gambling directed at US citizens illegal, most banks exercised a maximum of caution and stopped dealing with Intrade and similar sites. A few continued, including an online payment system called Neteller.com, which is British-owned and based in the Isle of Man. Its Canadian cofounders were arrested during a trip to the United States in 2007, and charged with conspiring to transfer funds with the intent to promote illegal gambling. This transfer involved several online gambling sites, not just Intrade. The two faced a potential twenty years in prison.

Prediction markets could shed their shaky legal status if the CFTC were to formally exempt small-stakes markets from prosecution, as they have for the IEM. In May 2007, a group of twenty high-profile researchers, which included Nobel economics laureates Kenneth Arrow, Daniel Kahneman, Vernon Smith, and Thomas Schelling, wrote to federal regulators with that suggestion.

The suggested exemption would allow a market on any meaningful economic, political, social, or medical event. The market would have to have a research focus and be nonprofit in nature. The size of individual investments would be capped—say to $2,500 per participant per market.

A second exemption would allow private businesses to run markets that were limited to employees, suppliers, and customers. A third would permit markets run by government agencies as part of their research on public policy issues such as epidemics, crime prevention, or terrorism.

Many of the submissions to the CFTC argued that an exemption should also cover sporting activities, if the investment was part of hedging on extreme outcomes. For example, local businesses in Buffalo, New York, might want to hedge against the negative economic impact on their already-beleaguered city if their National Football League team relocated to Toronto. But sports will almost certainly not be included; sports prediction looks too much like Las Vegas–style gambling.

The idea of a commodity market being first shunned and later embraced is not without precedent. Insurance markets were prohibited until the late nineteenth century because they were seen as a form of gambling. Once insurance was recognized as filling a useful function, it was exempted from gambling statutes.

Exemption would open the floodgates to US investor participation in prediction markets. During the 2008 presidential election campaign, Intrade handled 2.4 million Obama and McCain contracts, charging five cents per trade and earning $120,000. They probably earned an equal amount from interest on money held in investor accounts. John Delaney said that if the CFTC clarified their legal status, investment in election markets would increase twentyfold.

In November 2010, the CFTC said the exemption idea, which it calls "safe harbor," was still "under staff review." Without waiting for a CFTC ruling, the North American Derivatives Exchange (NADEX) petitioned the Commission for a "no action" letter to allow predictions trading only on US presidential elections and control of the House and Senate. NADEX is a relatively small futures exchange, trading about one million contracts each year in stock indices, currencies, and energy, compared with three billion contracts traded at the Chicago Mercantile Exchange. The outlook for the application is not promising. CFTC commissioner Bart Chilton commented, "Betting on elections is illegal even in Vegas." The Commission is expected to rule on the NADEX application by mid-2012, and that will be seen by the prediction markets community as its opinion on the whole idea of exemptions.

Until the CFTC acts, real-money markets are in a grey legal area. Play-money markets are presumed to be legal, and in-house markets with nominal prizes are in a "don't bother with" category, much the same as office football pools.

Would the DARPA Policy Analysis Markets on terrorism have been legal? It did not occur to DARPA officials to ask until very late in the process. When the issue was raised, well after PAM had been terminated, officials responded that their proposed market would have been an agency of the Department of Defense and thus have had immunity from federal prosecution—as though the Pentagon had decided to run a kind of national lottery.

A more serious long-term issue facing prediction markets is the possibility a market will trigger an insider trading violation for a publicly traded company. If Jane Smith sees a market price on the Best Buy intranet that suggests a key company initiative is facing serious but unannounced problems, or one on Merck's dashboard predicting that a new drug will be a blockbuster success, can she trade that company's shares on this information? Has she become an insider because she now has information that until now, only senior executives had? If she does trade, what obligation does this impose on the company?

A simple cost-benefit analysis suggests that prediction markets will be used on those topics of highest value to the corporation. These include product introductions, product pricing, geographic expansion, and mergers and acquisitions—exactly the information that creates movement in stock prices.

There are two obvious company responses to insider trading concerns: treat internal prediction market questions and prices as trade secrets, or make public the market securities offered and prices obtained in in-house markets. This would shelter the company from legal liability because insider trading relates only to material, nonpublic information. Releasing market results would, of course, make the same information available to competitors. These concerns do not apply to private company markets.

If the decision is that markets can't deal with any question where the result would be subject to financial disclosure, their usefulness declines a bit. That still leaves markets as a great tool to investigate new ideas, process improvements, key performance indicators, and product quality concerns.

Checklist for Starting a Prediction Market

If you want to initiate a prediction market from scratch within your organization, here is a checklist for getting started:

1. Find a market champion to develop the first market. She does not have to have a business school background or a quant background. Most of the prediction market champions I talk about in the book—Jim Lavoie, Joe Marino, and Fortune Elkins—had never gone to business school or learned about markets (Brian Jaedike is my exception). Knowledge dispensed in business schools comes bundled with a lot of conventional wisdom about how decisions are made in a hierarchical organization. If possible, start with an unconventional market champion.

2. Spend some time investing in a public market like Intrade, so you understand and can talk about the experience of taking part in a market. The champion should check the "Prediction Market Software" and "Prediction Market Sites Worth Following" sections that follow. Then experiment with available commercial software—at least Inkling, Consensus Point, and Hasbro/Monopoly—so you can discuss the technical aspects.

3. Prepare a presentation that includes three or four examples of successful markets involving a variety of businesses and questions.

4. Get your "air cover" in place. Make your presentation to the highest level in the company you can reach. Outline the first two or three proposed market topics (short-term events, and nothing on sales estimates or market shares!) and the budget. Ballpark esti-

mate: $3,000–$5,000 in out-of-pocket expenses, including modest prizes, will get you through a couple of test markets. This does not cover the time of a market champion and one or two IT people.

5. Try to anticipate all the perceived threats to existing fiefdoms. Sell the market idea to middle-management people and technical staff (separate presentations) before guerilla warfare can start. Emphasize that markets supplement the organization's existing strategy and research process, not supplant it.

6. A good starting position, whether you are challenged or not, is that markets are useful as a reality check on existing forecasts. When the two deviate, it may be because markets are real-time and incorporate information not available in the earlier study. Point out that deviation raises a red flag for forecasting staff that the issue warrants more study.

7. Contract with a software vendor for a trial period.

8. Run the initial market in one department or division only. Choose a site and questions that carry minimal political risks.

9. Decide who should participate in the test markets. Twenty traders are enough if they are interested, are active, and have diverse backgrounds. Enlist and fund some "noise" traders to inject provocative wagers and produce reactions from smarter investors. Decide how you will communicate during the market—a weekly e-mailed newsletter and update is a minimum.

10. If you are concerned about low participation, there is a solution that I haven't mentioned in the book: some consulting firms that run prediction markets compensate investors to create interest. PAM was originally designed to include a subsidy for early market participation. This seems to work, as long as the subsidy is not in a form that permits the market to be gamed—for example, by paying investors for each trade they make.

11. Get involvement from concerned middle-management people in choosing questions and setting market ranges. Avoid questions where bullying colleagues, nervous managers, or technical "experts" will be most tempted to influence others. Keep the market period short to maintain interest.

12. Use questions about areas where there is enough relevant information for the market to aggregate. Express the variables to be predicted in a precise way: "Gift certificate sales between September 15 and March 15, in dollars." Provide previous-year or other comparables.

13. Include fun questions about sports results or politics, but beware of garbage-in, garbage-out questions.

14. Decide on incentives to reward investors and to signal that the market is important—T-shirts, monetary awards, gift cards, entries in a draw for a trip, public recognition from the general manager, or some combination.

15. Investors and potential investors have to be told the outcome of markets. If they are not told, everyone is less motivated to take part in the next market. Investors need to know that management is paying attention—think of Best Buy assigning additional resources to the opening of a new store in Shanghai.

16. Decide how you will announce the winners and the consensus forecast, particularly if the prediction differs from what managers have previously said.

17. Launch the second set of market questions before you announce the outcome of the first round, to emphasize that this is an ongoing process.

Prediction Market Software

To set up a prediction market, you need software. As the use of markets has increased over the past decade, more software vendors have appeared, with more options and friendlier interfaces. There are three ways of getting started. The first option is to choose a vendor, purchase a software package plus consulting assistance, and host the market on your own system. This has the advantage of known costs and assured operation. The disadvantages are those found with any off-the-shelf software: higher front-end costs, ongoing support and licensing fees, and limited opportunity to customize.

The second alternative is to host a prediction market from a software vendor and run it on the vendor's system. This has the advantages of low front-end cost, no maintenance cost, limited need for technical expertise, and a short lead-time before you are up and running. Several vendors will let you run a free trial period if you ask, reducing front-end cost even further. Disadvantages of the vendor hosting the market are ongoing fees, limited opportunity to customize, and having company information stored outside your firewall on an outside system.

The third alternative is to build your own system, either from scratch or based on existing software that can be customized. This is what Google, Yahoo!, and HP have done. This option allows you to customize and add the features you want. The disadvantages are uncertain front-end costs and ongoing maintenance and support costs.

If you choose to purchase or host, or are looking for an existing system to customize, the prediction market software available offers some good options. The following list is probably incomplete and has a North American bias, but it includes the major suppliers. Firms are listed within categories, in alphabetical order. I have provided very brief descriptions for each site. Check them out yourself.

Commercial Prediction Software

Consensus Point (www.consensuspoint.com)

Consensus Point licenses its Foresight Prediction Market, which can be hosted either on its own system or on the client's. It offers different trading interfaces. The beginning interface asks questions about whether you believe the event will occur. You are then shown how to invest your trading currency. The next level of interface allows you to buy or sell shares. The advanced interface shows the buy-and-sell order book, with information on existing positions. There is a "confidence interface" that allows investors to indicate how much confidence they have in their answers to each question. Consensus Point clients include Best Buy, General Mills, General Electric Energy, and Motorola. It offers consulting services as well as software.

Crowdcast (www.crowdcast.com)

Crowdcast's principal business is running markets for corporate clients, to gather intelligence on questions such as when a product will ship and what the market share will be. It uses a combination of prediction markets and discussion forums to highlight risks and summarize investor logic on both sides of the market. There is a voting system for ranking ideas, which can then be turned into a prediction market. Clients include Boeing, General Motors, Hallmark, and Johnson & Johnson.

Inkling (www.inklingmarkets.com)

Inkling hosts corporate prediction markets and provides social networking and collaboration tools. Clients include P&G, Microsoft, Chevron, and the Institute for the Future. Inking offers a trading widget that employees can use to predict project completion metrics within Basecamp, a popular Web application for project management. It also offers a forty-five-day free software trial and special pricing for small businesses—starting at $39 per month for five or fewer questions.

Intrade (www.intrade.com)

Intrade, located in Dublin, has in a few cases licensed its commercial market software to organizations wanting to run large-scale markets. London's *Financial Times* uses the Intrade platform to run its FTPredict site.

Lumenogic (www.lumenogic.com)

Formerly the company NewsFutures, which had been in existence since 2000. Lumenogic specializes in organizing prediction markets and other online competitions for corporate customers; its recent publicized success was with the US Air Force, getting feedback from lower-echelon workers on drone cameras and radar systems.

Nosco (www.nosco.dk)

Nosco is a Danish company offering a form of prediction market software for idea management, and a consulting service. Clients include Ramboll, Velux, DSB, and Microsoft.

Pro:kons (www.prokons.com)

Pro:kons is a Swiss site offering prediction market and consensus-building software. Clients include Telfonica and Mobilkom Austria. Its software functions in French, German, Italian, and English.

Qmarkets (www.Qmarkets.net)

Qmarkets is headquartered in Israel, and produces prediction market and idea management software. Customers are smaller enterprises and include Enterprise Development Group and Datalynx.

Rite-Solutions/Hasbro (www.rite-solutions.com)

Whatever other software you consider, compare it with the Rite-Solutions Mutual Fun Market, or Rite-Solutions/Hasbro Monopoly, both discussed in chapter 1. I'm not sure whether a precondition for using this software is a management culture of complete openness to market results. You decide. At time of writing, the software was not yet being offered; check the Rite-Solutions website or Google the terms.

Spigit (www.spigit.com)

Spigit is a Web-based social innovation tool with blogs, wikis, surveys, and prediction markets. Spigit uses mathematical models to assign investors different rankings or weights for their ideas and comments, based on their expertise and past successes. Clients include Farmer's Insurance, Southwest Airlines, Pfizer, and Lloyds Bank.

Open Source Prediction Software

Zocalo (www.zocalo.sourceforge.net)

Zocalo is a free prediction market software tool kit produced by Chris Hibbert of commerce.net. It is open source on a Java development platform. Hibbert is available to consult on implementation if needed. This has been used successfully with several PhD and MS theses. There are lots of useful links on structuring markets.

Prediction Market Sites Worth Following

Real-Money Prediction Exchanges

Intrade (www.intrade.com)

Intrade operates the largest commercial, real-money prediction market, with a turnover of just under $100 million a year. Headquartered in Dublin, Intrade began trading in 2002. The site lists 160 markets at one time, and trades 200,000 contracts a day. It has 82,000 investors from 140 countries, most from the United States. Intrade provides free real-time transparent price discovery information to millions of people observing the site.

While Intrade's slant is toward financial issues, contracts cover a wide range: political races, bird flu epidemics, Arctic oil drilling, climate change, commodity prices, economic numbers, entertainment awards, US Homeland Security issues, and who will win *American Idol*. This is a good site to get ideas on what fun markets can be offered on an in-house market. Intrade will list a contract on almost any future event its members would like to see traded.

Price information on event markets has been requested from Intrade by organizations as diverse as the US Navy, the Federal Reserve Bank of New York, the European Central Bank, the Bank of Japan, CNN, CNBC, and Fox Television. A long list of global media businesses, including the *New York Times*, *Wall Street Journal*, *Washington Post*, *Financial Times*, *Economist*, and *Bloomberg* cite Intrade event market information.

Iowa Electronic Markets (www.biz.uiowa.edu/iem)

This is a group of real-money markets operated by the University of Iowa's Tippie College of Business. The markets are run for research and educational purposes; most are open to nonuniversity investors. Markets are available on political races, company earnings per share, Federal Reserve monetary policy, and other topics. Traders are limited to a $500 position.

Play-Money Prediction Markets

NewsFutures (www.lumenogic.com)

For years the NewsFutures US site offered markets on current events, politics, finance, sports, and questions as diverse as whether US troops will actually be out of Iraq by a certain date and whether Nicolas Sarkozy and Carla Bruni will divorce. The company has now merged with another consultant and been renamed Lumenogic. The combined firm places much less emphasis on prediction markets and public interest topics.

Foresight Exchange Prediction Markets (www.ideosphere.com)

Foresight is a public, play-money market that trades in political, finance, science, and technology events suggested by clients. It predicted that a computer would defeat Garry Kasparov at chess, two years before it happened. Foresight allows trading on long-term issues from resignation of political figures to a major earthquake in the western United States. Foresight is affiliated with Consensus Point.

Hollywood Stock Exchange (www.hsx.com)

The Hollywood Stock Exchange is a play-money market in the future success of new movies, actors, directors, and other film-related issues, such as who will win Academy Awards. This is the biggest play-money market in the world, and probably the most democratic.

Inkling Public Marketplace (www.inklingmarkets.com)

Primarily a corporate prediction market site, Inking also runs a play-money market with financial, political, movie, and sports topics.

Media Predict (www.mediapredict.com)

Media Predict offers markets on media, television plots, upcoming movies, and more.

The simExchange (www.thesimexchange.com)

The simExchange runs markets on the success of new video games, allowing participants to buy securities on which games will sell more or less than predicted.

Iowa Health Prediction Market (www.iehm.uiowa.edu/iehm/index.html)

The Iowa Health Prediction Market is a research project at the University of Iowa using prediction markets for disease surveillance in time for the information to be clinically useful.

Apart from the internal corporate prediction markets mentioned in this book, there are many other companies that use markets, the outcomes of which sometimes appear in the public domain. Enter the company name and "prediction markets" into the Google search line for the following and see what comes up: Abbott Labs, Arcelor Mittal, Cisco Systems, Corning, Electronic Arts, Frito Lay, General Electric, Intel, InterContinental Hotels, Masterfoods, Microsoft, Motorola, Nokia, Pfizer, Qualcomm, Siemens, and others mentioned in these pages.

Further Reading

Chapter 1: The Mutual Fun Market

Lavoie, Jim. "The Innovation Engine at Rite-Solutions: Lessons from the CEO." *Journal of Prediction Markets* 1 (2009): 1–11.

Leadbeater, Charles. *We-Think: The Power of Mass Creativity*. London: Profile Books, 2008.

Taylor, William C. *Practically Radical: Not-So-Crazy Ways to Transform Your Company, Shake Up Your Industry, and Challenge Yourself*. New York: William Morrow, 2011. This has a section on Lavoie, Marino, and Rite-Solutions.

Chapter 2: What Are These Prediction Markets?

Hanson, Robin, Ryan Oprea, and David Porter. *Information Aggregation and Manipulation in an Experimental Market*. Working paper, George Mason University, Fairfax, VA, 2006. http://hanson.gmu.edu/biastest.pdf.

Hayek, F. A. "The Use of Knowledge in Society." *American Economic Review* 35 (1945): 519–530. This is a classic article, and provides great background.

Howe, Jeff. *Crowdsourcing: Why the Power of the Crowd Is Driving the Future of Business*. New York: Crown Business, 2008. This explains how companies from Hewlett-Packard to start-up iStockphoto use digital crowds to drive new products and increase business.

Chapter 3: Sports and Movie Markets

Crafts, N. F. R. "Some Evidence of Insider Knowledge in Horse Race Betting in Britain." *Economica* (1985): 295–304. This compares track handicappers' morning line on horse races with predictions from pari-mutuel betting.

Figlewski, S. "Subjective Information and Market Efficiency in a Betting Market." *Journal of Political Economy* (1979): 75–88. This compares success rates of horse race handicappers and pari-mutuel bettors.

Hamel, Gary, with Bill Breen. *The Future of Management*. Boston: Harvard Business School Press, 2007.

Hoerl, Arthur, and Herbert Fallin. "Reliability of Subjective Evaluations in a High Incentive Situation." *Journal of the Royal Statistical Society* (July 1974): 227–230. This offers statistical evidence of how hard it is to outperform the collective of bettors involved in setting pari-mutuel odds.

Mauboussin, Michael. *More Than You Know: Finding Financial Wisdom in Unconventional Places.* New York: Columbia Business School Press, 2008.

Nocera, Joseph. "The Oscar Experiment." *Fortune,* March 22, 2004.

Sauer, R. D. "The Economics of Wagering Markets." *Journal of Economic Literature* (1998): 2021–2064. This provides evidence on how well pari-mutuel odds match with the long-term outcomes of horse races.

Smith, Michael A., David Paton, and Leighton Vaughan Williams. "Do Bookmakers Possess Superior Skills to Bettors in Predicting Outcomes?" *Journal of Economic Behavior and Organization* 71 (August 2009), 539–549. This article compares two sets of odds for the same UK horse races, one set from bookmakers, the other from pari-mutuel wagering.

Chapter 4: Election Markets

Berg, J. E., R. Forsythe, F. D. Nelson, and T. A. Rietz. "Results from a Dozen Years of Election Futures Markets Research." In *Handbook of Experimental Economic Results,* edited by C. R. Plott and V. L. Smith. Amsterdam: North Holland, 2003. This offers a history of the Iowa Electronic Markets.

Forsythe, Robert, Forrest Nelson, George R. Neumann, and Jack Wright. "Anatomy of an Experimental Political Stock Market." *American Economic Review* 82 (December 1992): 1148.

Rhode, Paul W., and Koleman Strumpf. *Historical Political Futures Markets: An International Perspective.* Working paper, National Bureau of Economic Research, Washington, DC, October 2008. www.nber.org/papers/w14377. This is the source of the discussion of the early history of waging on the selection of officers in the Catholic Church.

Stix, Gary. "Super Tuesday: Markets Predict Outcomes Better than Polls." *Scientific American,* March 2008, 38–45.

Sunstein, Cass. "Group Judgments: Deliberations, Statistical Means, and Information Markets." *New York University Law Review* 80 (2005): 962–1049.

Surowiecki, James. *The Wisdom of Crowds: Why the Many Are Smarter than the Few, and How Collective Wisdom Shapes Business, Economies, Societies, and Nations.* New York: Doubleday, 2004.

Wolfers, Justin, and Eric Zitzewitz. "Experimental Political Betting Markets and the 2004 Election." *The Economists' Voice* 1, no. 2 (2004). www.bepress.com/ev/vol1/iss2/art1.

———. "Prediction Markets." *Journal of Economic Perspectives* 18 (2004): 107–126.

Chapter 5: Estimation Markets

Meirowitz, Adam, and Joshua A. Tucker. "Learning from Terrorism Markets." *Perspectives on Politics* (June 2004): 331–336. This is the source of the "use of a prediction market" experiment for *Who Wants to Be a Millionaire.*

Page, Scott E. *The Difference: How the Power of Diversity Creates Better Groups, Firms, Schools, and Societies.* Princeton, NJ: Princeton University Press, 2007. Page's work provides a framework for explaining the importance of diversity and goes beyond anecdotal examples to provide a theoretical underpinning for why prediction markets work.

Sunstein, Cass R. *Going to Extremes: How Like Minds Unite and Divide.* New York: Oxford University Press, 2008. Sunstein discusses why we should mistrust human judgment in everything from politics to business, because wrongheadedness gets worse when people get together in groups and the strongest opinion prevails.

———. *Infotopia: How Many Minds Produce Knowledge.* New York: Oxford University Press, 2006, 45–46.

Chapter 6: What Can Prediction Markets Replace?

Baker, Stephen. *The Numerati.* New York: Houghton Mifflin Harcourt, 2008.

Kahneman, Daniel. *Thinking, Fast and Slow.* New York: Farrar, Straus & Giroux, 2011. Kahneman, a winner of the Nobel Prize in Economics, provides an encyclopedic coverage and wonderful narrative of the mistakes we make in conscious and unconscious decision making.

Mauboussin, Michael. *Mauboussin on Strategy* (newsletter from Legg Mason Capital Management, New York), September 1, 2009. This includes the discussion of his voting to bring a person into the organization (page 8).

———. *Think Twice: Harnessing the Power of Intuition.* Boston: Harvard Business Press, 2009. Mauboussin contrasts prediction markets to the approach in Malcolm Gladwell's book *Blink* (New York: Basic Books, 2007), in which Gladwell advises faith in intuition based on experience. Mauboussin argues that intuition works well in stable environments where cause-and-effect relationships are clear, but says these conditions are rare in a complex world. He advances a good argument for using the wisdom of diverse crowds, rather than experts.

Orrell, David. *The Future of Everything: The Science of Prediction: From Wealth and Weather to Chaos and Complexity.* New York: Thunder's Mouth Press, 2007.

Payne, John, and Arnold Wood. "Individual Decision Making and Group Decision Processes." *Journal of Psychology and Financial Markets* 3, no. 2 (2002): 94–101.

Senate Select Committee on Intelligence. *U.S. Intelligence Community's Prewar Intelligence Assessments on Iraq.* Report of the 108th Congress, July 2004. This contains the discussion of biases in the conclusion that Iraq had weapons of mass destruction programs.

Sunstein, Cass R. "Group Judgments: Statistical Means, Deliberation, and Prediction Markets." *New York University Law Review* 80 (2005): 962–1049. This is a more technical version of the material in Sunstein's *Infotopia*.

————. *Infotopia: How Many Minds Produce Knowledge.* New York: Oxford University Press, 2006. The book looks at the "wisdom of the many" and "groupthink," in a more analytic way than Surowiecki's *Wisdom of Crowds.* Sunstein discusses wikis, open source software, blogs, *Wikipedia*, spurring technological advances, and prediction markets. Highly recommended.

Tetlock, Philip. *Expert Political Judgment.* Princeton, NJ: Princeton University Press, 2005.

Chapter 7: Google

Berg, Joyce E., George R. Neumann, and Thomas A. Rietz. *Searching for Google's Value: Using Prediction Markets to Forecast Market Capitalization Prior to an Initial Public Offering.* Working paper, Henry B. Tippie College of Business, University of Iowa, 2008. This is a fairly technical discussion of valuing Google's IPO.

Brin, Sergey, and Lawrence Page. *The Anatomy of a Large-Scale Hypertextual Web Search Engine.* www.infolab.stanford.edu/backrub/google.html. This is the classic article on the Google search engine, and perhaps the most read and reproduced article in the annals of computing science. The original is better left to those with a math and technology background. A more readable version can be found on Google at www.google.com/corporate/tech.html.

Cowgill, Bo. *Putting Crowd Wisdom to Work.* www.googleblog.blogspot.com/2005/09/putting-crowd-wisdom-to-work.html. This is Cowgill's presentation on why Google should have a prediction market.

Ginsberg, Jeremy, Matthew H. Mohebbi, Rajan S. Patel, Lynnette Brammer, Mark S. Smolinski, and Larry Brilliant. "Detecting Influenza Epidemics Using Search Engine Query Data." *Nature* 19 (2009), 1012–1015.

Iyer, Bala, and Thomas H. Davenport. "Reverse Engineering Google's Innovation Machine." *Harvard Business Review,* April 2008, 58–68.

Chapter 10: Boardroom Markets

Abramowicz, Michael, and M. Todd Henderson. *Prediction Markets for Corporate Governance.* Law & Economics Olin Working Paper No. 307, University of Chicago Law School, 2007. www.ssrn.com/sol3/papers.cfm?abstract_id=928896. This is a good overview of the use of prediction markets in corporate governance.

Collins, Jim. *How the Mighty Fall . . . And Why Some Companies Never Give In.* New York: HarperCollins, 2009.

Kambil, Ajit. "Betting on a New Market." *Trends and Ideas,* October 2003. This describes the HP emissions market.

Kelly, Kate. *Street Fighters: The Last 72 Hours of Bear Stearns, the Toughest Firm on Wall Street.* New York: Portfolio, 2009. This tells the story of the firm's executives ignoring internal warnings about the value of their mortgage-backed bonds and derivatives.

Taleb, Nassim Nicholas. *The Black Swan: The Impact of the Highly Improbable.* New York: Random House, 2007.

Chapter 11: Way-Outside-the-Box Markets: Casting Calls and Epidemiology

Hahn, Robert W., and Paul C. Tetlock. "Making Development Work." *Policy Review* 132 (2005): 27–38.

Pisani, Elizabeth. *The Wisdom of Whores: Bureaucrats, Brothels, and the Business of AIDS.* New York: Viking, 2008.

Polgreen, Philip M., Forrest D. Nelson, and George R. Neumann. "Use of Prediction Markets to Forecast Infectious Disease Activity." *Clinical Infectious Diseases* 44 (2007). www.journals.uchicago.edu/doi/abs/10.1086/510427.

Chapter 12: Further Outside the Box: Terrorism Markets

Brown, Dan. *The Lost Symbol.* New York: Doubleday, 2009.

Hanson, Robin. "Designing Real Terrorism Futures." *Public Choice* 128 (2006): 257–274.

Looney, Robert E. "DARPA's Policy Analysis Market for Intelligence: Outside the Box or Off the Wall?" *International Journal of Intelligence and Counterintelligence* 17 (2004): 405–419. The article reproduced several windows from the original PAM website, which was at www.PolicyAnalysisMarket.org, but has now been taken down.

Senate Select Committee on Intelligence. *U.S. Intelligence Community's Prewar Intelligence Assessments on Iraq.* Report of the 108th Congress, July 2004.

Wyden, Ron, and Byron Dorgan. *Wyden, Dorgan Call for Immediate Halt to Tax-Funded 'Terror Market' Scheme,* July 28, 2003. www.wyden.senate.gov/media/2003/07282003_terrormarket.html. This is the open letter to Rear Admiral John Poindexter in which the two members of the Senate complain about PAM being a "terror market."

Yeh, Puong Fei. *CSI: Using Prediction Markets to Enhance US Intelligence Capabilities, a "Standard & Poors 500 Index" for Intelligence.* www.cia.gov/library/center-for-the-study-of-intelligence/csi-publications-studies. This is a CIA briefing paper on the DARPA project and its demise. The URL links to a heavily edited version.

Chapter 13: Government Markets

Abramowicz, Michael B. *Predictocracy: Market Mechanisms for Public and Private Decision Making.* New Haven, CT: Yale University Press, 2007. This is a book-length treatment on innovative ways of using decision markets to advance a system of republican government.

Berg, Joyce E., and T. A. Rietz. "Prediction Markets as Decision Support Systems." *Information Systems Frontiers* 5 (2003): 79–93.

Brown, Dan. *The Lost Symbol.* New York: Doubleday, 2009. One of Brown's fictional characters, Trish Dunne, discusses writing meta systems software to permit crunching enormous data fields to analyze civilian e-mail, telephone, and fax messages (beginning on page 74).

Cherry, Miriam A., and Robert L. Rogers. "Tiresias and the Justices: Using Information Markets to Predict Supreme Court Decisions." *Northwestern University Law Review* 100, no. 3 (2006): 1141–1196. Tiresias is an oracle in Greek mythology, a character in *Oedipus Rex* and in *Antigone.*

Fox, James Alan. *Forecasting Crime Data.* New York: Lexington Books, 1978. This gives an overview of more traditional statistical approaches to determining crime rates.

Hahn, Robert W., and Paul C. Tetlock. *How Information Markets Could Change the Policy World.* Washington, DC: AEI-Brookings Joint Center for Regulatory Studies, 2004.

Hanson, Robin D. "Shall We Vote on Values but Bet on Beliefs?" *Journal of Political Philosophy* (2007). http://hanson.gmu.edu/futarchy.pdf.

Henderson, M. Todd, Justin Wolfers, and Eric Zitzewitz. *Predicting Crime.* Olin Working Paper No. 402, University of Chicago Law School (2008). www.ssrn.com/sol3/papers.cfm?abstract_id=1118931. This is a great discussion of the potential of markets in predicting crime.

National Aeronautics and Space Administration. *Report of the* Columbia *Accident Investigation Board.* Washington, DC: Government Printing Office, 2003, 97–204. www.nasa.gov/columbia/home/CAIB_vol1.html. This is the full report on the *Columbia* disaster.

Chapter 14: Long-Term Markets

Kurzweil, Ray. *The Singularity Is Near: When Humans Transcend Biology.* New York: Viking Press, 2005.

Chapter 15: When No One Wants to Know

Lewis, Michael. "Wall Street on the Tundra." *Vanity Fair,* April 2009. This is a hilarious account of the collective madness that led to the 2008 de facto bankruptcy of Iceland.

Lewis, Michael, and David Einhorn. "The End of the Financial World as We Know It." *New York Times,* January 4, 2009. This is one of the best articles I know in explaining the 2008 crash and how it came about.

McCreary, Lew. "How to Kill Bad Projects," *Harvard Business Review Editors Blog,* http://discussionleader.hbsp.com/hbreditors/2008/06/how_to_kill_bad_projects_1.html.

McDonald, Lawrence G., and Patrick Robinson. *A Colossal Failure of Common Sense: The Inside Story of the Collapse of Lehman Brothers.* New York: Crown Press, 2009.

Taleb, Nassim Nicholas. *The Black Swan: The Impact of the Highly Improbable.* New York: Random House, 2007.

Chapter 16: More Red Flags Than Beijing

Markopolos, Harry. *No One Would Listen: A True Financial Thriller.* Hoboken, NJ: Wiley, 2010. This is Markopolos's account of a nine-year struggle to have the Securities and Exchange Commission investigate Bernard Madoff.

Chapter 17: Finding the Scorpion

Johnson, Stephen. *Silent Steel: The Mysterious Death of the Nuclear Attack Sub USS* Scorpion. New York: John Wiley, 2006.

Maloney, Michael, and Harold Mulherin. "The Complexity of Price Discovery in an Efficient Market: The Stock Market Reaction to the *Challenger* Crash." *Journal of Corporate Finance* 9 (2003): 453–479. This discusses the NYSE prediction market success mentioned at the beginning of the chapter.

Offley, Ed. Scorpion *Down: Sunk by the Soviets, Buried by the Pentagon.* New York: Basic Books, 2007.

———. "The USS *Scorpion:* Mystery of the Deep." *Seattle Post-Intelligencer,* May 21, 1998. www.members.aol.com/bear317d/scorpion.htm. Offley specializes in military issues, and has been twice nominated for the Pulitzer Prize for his writing.

Sewell, Kenneth, and Jerome Preisler. *All Hands Down: The True Story of the Soviet Attack on the USS* Scorpion. New York: Simon & Schuster, 2008.

Postscript and Acknowledgments

Thompson, Donald N. *Marketing Management in Turkey: Cases and Challenges.* Ankara: Gazi Kitabevi, 2006. This contains the student prediction market experiment that is mentioned in the chapter (pages 234–239); an expanded version appears in the Turkish edition, *Turkiya'deki Pazarlama Vak'alari: Zorluklar ve Firsatlar* (pages 283–288).

Index

About the Author

Donald N. Thompson is an economist and professor of marketing and strategy at the Schulich School of Business at York University in Toronto. He has taught at Harvard Business School and the London School of Economics. Thompson is the author of nine books, including *The $12 Million Stuffed Shark: The Curious Economics of Contemporary Art* (Palgrave Macmillan, 2008), which has been published in eleven languages.